Men-at-Arms • 377

Luftwaffe Air & Ground Crew 1939–45

Robert F Stedman · Illustrated by Mike Chappell

Series editor Martin Windrow

First published in Great Britain in 2002 by Osprey Publishing,
Midland House, West Way, Botley, Oxford OX2 0PH, UK
443 Park Avenue South, New York, NY 10016, USA
Email: info@ospreypublishing.com

CIP Data for this publication is available from the British Library

ISBN 978-1-84176-404-7

Typeset in Helvetica Neue and ITC New Baskerville
Editor: Martin Windrow
Design: Alan Hamp
Index by Alan Rutter
Originated by Magnet Harlequin, Uxbridge, UK
Printed in China through World Print Ltd.

08 09 10 11 12 13 12 11 10 9 8 7 6 5 4

FOR A CATALOGUE OF ALL BOOKS PUBLISHED BY
OSPREY MILITARY AND AVIATION PLEASE CONTACT:

NORTH AMERICA
Osprey Direct, C/o Random House Distribution Center, 400 Hahn Road,
Westminster, MD 21157, USA
E-mail: info@ospreydirect.com

ALL OTHER REGIONS
Osprey Direct UK, P.O. Box 140, Wellingborough, Northants, NN8 2FA, UK
E-mail: info@ospreydirect.co.uk

www.ospreypublishing.com

Dedication

Dedicated to the memory of my uncle, Malcolm John Hall
Myers (1943–2000), with whom I enjoyed many educational, witty and
often surreal conversations. A few more would have been even
better.
Also to the memory of all the men and women of the Luftwaffe
who lost their lives in the service of their country.

Acknowledgements

I wish to express my sincerest thanks to my favourite author and
great friend, Martin J.Brayley, for his constant support, advice and
encouragement throughout this project – despite being busy with
even more titles of his own. To Mark Taylor, for his many hours of
outstanding work in identifying aircraft types, researching and
locating units for the colour plates, and altogether being the best
friend a chap could ever have. To Hayley Morris for devoting so
much of her time, translation skills, technical support and patience
during countless re-writes and proof-readings. Special thanks are
owed to Martin Windrow, for having faith in me in the first place.

I have received much co-operation from fellow collectors who
graciously allowed me to 'cross-examine' items from their
collections; chief among these is Mike Wenger of Raleigh,
N.Carolina, whose exhaustive work to record details and
chronology of Luftwaffe flight suits has greatly assisted my own
research. For their generous assistance with photographs and
information I must also thank MJB, Aldo Carrer, Mark
Dial, Deborah & Russel Doherty, Manfred Griehl, Tom Gulliver,
Kenneth Keilholz, Steve Kiddle, Jeanette Leib, Lionel Leventhal of
Greenhill Books, Hans Obert, Werner Palinckx, Wolfgang Schilling,
Franz Selinger, LAC Keith Stedman, Lee Timmins, Paul West, and
Dr Willisch of the Luftwaffenmuseum, Berlin; and Phil Burchell, for
the emergency loan of his computer. Photographs not otherwise
credited are from the author's collection.

The publishers are grateful to Cassell & Co and Malcolm
McGregor for permission to reproduce the latter's artwork in the
charts on pages 13, 17 & 44, which originally appeared in Brian L.
Davis, *Uniforms and Insignia of the Luftwaffe* (2 vols.), 1991 &1995.

Author's Note

It has been my intention to address a few long-standing and oft-
repeated myths in the field of Luftwaffe 'uniformology'. Principal
among these is the development of the 1934 flight suit and its so-
called 'escape vent'. It is generally accepted that its purpose was
to ease the rapid removal of the suit in an (unspecified) emergency.
As the vent runs from the waist and terminates below the collar,
escape through this modest opening is simply impossible. An alternative theory suggests that it permitted relatively painless access to
a casualty's wound – but in practice such access is limited to the
left side of the torso, whereas the main zip effectively cuts the suit
in half. It must be remembered that a parachute and life vest would
first have to be removed from the casualty, followed by a forceful
tug to actuate the system – all of which would hardly be conducive
to 'painless access'.

Designations used for the two-piece flight suits are at present
unconfirmed, but follow the established system. These are included
for ease of reference.

LUFTWAFFE AIR & GROUND CREW 1939–45

Late 1934: the 22-year-old Adolf Galland in the blue-grey uniform of a pilot-qualified Deutscher Luftsport Verband (DLV) Flieger; note the rhomboid-shaped collar patches with rank *'Schwingen'*, soon to be adopted by the Luftwaffe. Galland first came to prominence as a ground attack and fighter pilot with the Legion Condor in Spain where, by the fall of the Republic in March 1939, many of the Jagdflieger who would become household names in 1940 – e.g. Galland, Günther Lutzow, Werner Mölders and Walter Oesau – had already become aces, and in the process had developed the most up-to-date fighter tactics in the world. Regular rotation of personnel to Spain gave a large number of airmen of all branches invaluable combat and command experience denied to their early opponents in World War II. German airmen in Spain claimed 386 enemy aircraft shot down, for 232 aircraft and 226 men lost. (Private collection)

INTRODUCTION

THE 1919 TREATY OF VERSAILLES banned German military aviation, but secret agreements between Germany and the USSR in 1923 established clandestine facilities at Lipetsk, Russia. In the 1930s the Deutscher Luftsports Verband (German Air Sports Association, DLV) also trained future military aircrews at the deceptively misnamed 'Zentrale der Verkehrs Fliegerschule' (Central Commercial Pilots' School). In February 1935, Hitler publicly announced the formation of the new Luftwaffe ('air arm'). His long-time collaborator Hermann Göring, a charismatic but militarily limited ex-Great War fighter pilot, was given chief command with the rank of Reichsmarschall – a role for which he would later prove spectacularly ill-qualified. For both operational and economic reasons priority was given to the creation of a tactical air force suitable for close support of ground offensives during a short, aggressive war, with a 'general purpose' medium bomber fleet rather than long-range strategic bombers.

The purpose of this book is to detail and illustrate Luftwaffe uniforms, work clothing and flying kit, and there is no space here for even a summarised history of the events of Germany's war in the air. (Readers are directed to the Osprey Aviation list, of which the most relevant titles are listed on the inside back cover of this book.) However, a brief list of the main campaigns may help put the uniform information and illustrations in context:

In July 1936 the **Spanish Civil War** broke out and, spurred by the prospect of Soviet support for the Republic, Hitler acceded to the Nationalist Gen. Franco's appeal for aid. The German volunteer corps or 'Legion Condor' had a strong air element, and the war provided invaluable opportunities to test machines and tactics and to accustom personnel to combat. This practical 'edge' contributed greatly to German victories in the **Blitzkrieg** campaigns of 1939 and 1940 against Poland, Norway, Denmark, France and the Low Countries and British expeditionary air forces. Although suffering significant casualties, Luftwaffe ground attack and bomber units greatly assisted the rapid advances of armoured and motorised troops, and the Messerschmitt Bf109 fighter units achieved air supremacy.

In July–October 1940 daytime operations to destroy the Royal Air Force (the **Battle of Britain**) in preparation for an invasion came close to success, but finally failed with heavy loss. The Luftwaffe switched to night bombing of British cities, ports and industrial targets; this **Blitz** of November 1940–May 1941 caused great damage and some 85,000 civilian casualties but brought little military advantage.

In 1941 the successes of the Western Blitzkrieg were replicated on a smaller scale in the **Balkans, Mediterranean and North Africa**, mainly against the RAF and Royal Navy. From June 1941 the invasion of the **USSR** brought staggering early success; the Luftwaffe completely outclassed the Red Air Force in quality of equipment and aircrew skills, and vast numbers of Russian aircraft were destroyed. During **1942**, however, the strain of fighting on **three fronts** simultaneously began to tell; Britain was no longer alone. The first USAAF daylight raids across the Channel began in August, and early losses did not deter a steadily increasing effort. During the summer a strengthened RAF Desert Air Force outnumbered Rommel's air support in Africa, while his vital supply lines from Italy were ravaged. In Russia the Red Air Force, buying time by dogged sacrifice, was slowly increasing in numbers and capability. The turn of 1942–43 brought catastrophic defeat in Africa and at Stalingrad, costing many aircraft and experienced crews. The weakened Luftwaffe would have little serious effect on military operations in **Italy** in 1943–45.

In early 1943 Luftwaffe fighter units were already being pulled back from Russia and the Mediterranean to help defend Germany against the **US 8th Air Force daylight offensive**. This battle of attrition intensified, and from winter 1943/44 US escort fighters had the range to accompany the Flying Fortresses all the way to Berlin and back. The German bomber fleet had been ground away to almost nothing, and many bomber aircrew were retrained on other aircraft; the heavy fighter ('destroyer') squadrons were largely retrained as night fighters to counter the RAF's massive **night bombing campaign** against German cities and factories.

While dwindling Luftwaffe fighter and ground attack squadrons continued to support German armies fighting a long and bitter defensive battle on the Eastern Front, the Western Allies opened another front by landing in **Normandy** in June 1944. They enjoyed air superiority from the first, and in the battles above their rapidly advancing

armies many irreplaceable Luftwaffe veterans were lost. German aircraft production actually increased toward the end of the war; but the shortage of experienced pilots, and of fuel, grew steadily more crippling as the Luftwaffe tried simultaneously to support retreating German armies in the West and East and to defend the Reich against the Allied bomber armadas. New weapons – such as the world's first operational jet fighter, the Messerschmitt Me262 – proved too few, and far too late.

By 8 May 1945, over 97,000 members of the Luftwaffe were recorded as dead, missing or wounded. Many combat airmen fell into despair upon discovering the crimes that had been committed behind the shield of their courage. Like their Allied counterparts, the great majority had been driven by a desire to serve their country, and to experience the ultimate test of self, rather than by ideology. Most of the men who faced them in the skies regarded them with nothing but respect.

COMMAND ORGANISATION

The operational branch of the Reichsluftfahrt Ministerium (national air ministry, RLM, accounting for 25,000 personnel in 1939) was the Oberkommando der Luftwaffe (air force high command, OKL). Under OKL the Luftwaffe was initially divided into four consecutively numbered regional Luftflotten (air fleets), later augmented by three more. Each Luftflotte commander was responsible for all air and supporting operations within that territory, although a subordinate Jagdführer (fighter leader – 'Jafü') supervised fighter operations. Each self-contained fleet was divided into several Luftgaue (air districts) and Fliegerkorps (flying corps). The Luftgau, staffed by a Generalmajor and 50 to 150 officers and men, provided permanent administrative and logistical structures and resources for each airfield. The Fliegerkorps was responsible for all operational matters, including deployment, air traffic, ordnance and maintenance. This flexible system enabled rapid preparedness for any attached 'visiting' flight unit from the moment of its arrival, unencumbered by a separate administrative element. The entire airfield staff would thereupon become subordinate to the commanding officer of that unit.

Luftflotten (HQ), areas of operation: principal campaigns

Luftflotte 1 (Berlin), N & E Germany: Poland 1939, North Russia.
Luftflotte 2 (Brunswick), NW Germany: Western Front 1939, Battle of Britain, Central Russia, Italy, Africa, Mediterranean.

Luftflotte 3 (Munich), SW Germany: Western Front 1939, Battle of Britain, invasion of Europe. *Luftflotte 4* (Vienna), SE Germany: Poland 1939, Balkans, South Russia, Hungary, Slovakia. *Luftflotte 5* (Oslo), Norway, Finland & northern Russia: Arctic front, North Russia. *Luftflotte 6* (Poland; moved to Brussels, Smolensk & Crimea late 1941), Central Russia: Poland, Slovakia, Bohemia-Moravia, Croatia. *Luftwaffe Zentral* (Berlin), renamed *Luftflotte Reich* on 5 February 1944. Home air defence, Denmark, East Prussia, Channel Islands, Norway, Hungary.

July 1940: a bespectacled *Luftwaffe-Sonderführer* (administrative official, equivalent to Major), visits an airfield in the West. Many of these hostilities-only personnel, whose appointment freed other officers for active service, had little or no military training. Trouser piping and collar patches – the latter without line officers' rank *Schwingen* – were in *karmesinrot* (crimson) Waffenfarbe. The rank of the Feldwebel (left) is accentuated by white *Ärmelstreifen* sleeve stripes adopted from May 1935 for work-wear and protective clothing, which at this date included the *Fliegerbluse* – note that it does not yet display the breast eagle.

COMPOSITION

Aircrew

Flight personnel constituted one of the smaller branches, numbering only some 50,000 in 1939. The largest autonomous unit was the Geschwader (wing), named and equipped for its mission (i.e. fighter, dive-bomber, bomber, etc.) and identified by Arabic numerals (e.g., Jagdgeschwader 1 or JG 1, Stukageschwader 2 or StG 2, Kampfgeschwader 3 or KG 3, etc.). Some Geschwadern bore additional 'honour titles', e.g. Jagdgeschwader 2 'Richthofen'.

The Stab (staff) flight of four aircraft under the 'Geschwaderkommodore' – usually an Oberst, Oberstleutnant or Major – commanded three or occasionally four Gruppen (groups), each with about 30 aircraft including a Stab element of three, and identified by Roman numerals (e.g. II Gruppe of JG 1, abbreviated to II./JG 1). Each was led by a Major or Hauptmann designated as 'Gruppenkommandeur'. Each Gruppe comprised three Arabic-numbered Staffeln (squadrons), each Staffel of nine aircraft being led by a 'Staffelkapitän', who might be a Hauptmann, an Oberleutnant or, after heavy casualties, even a Leutnant. The Gruppe number was omitted in abbreviation, as this could be deduced from the Staffel number (e.g. 5 Staffel, II Gruppe, JG 1 was designated 5./JG 1). Ergänzungsgruppen (replacement training groups) were later added to each bomber Geschwader, and sometimes a temporary V Gruppe, giving an average strength of c.90–120 aircraft. Gruppen were quite often transferred from one Geschwader to another and renumbered.

Flight unit designations

Jagdgeschwader (JG): 'hunting' (single-engined fighter)
Kampfgeschwader (KG): 'battle' (level bomber)
Kampfgeschwader zur besonderen Verwendung (KG zbV):'battle wing for special purposes', until May 1943 when redesignated –
Transportgeschwader (TG)
Kampfschulgeschwader (KSG): 'battle school' (bomber training)
Lehrgeschwader (LG): Advanced training, demonstration & tactical development
Luftlandegeschwader (LLG): air-landing (glider)
Nachtjagdgeschwader (NJG): night fighter

Sturzkampf(Stuka)geschwader (StG): dive bomber; later redesignated –

Schlachtgeschwader (SchG): 'slaughter' (ground attack), abbreviation changed to SG in October 1943

Schnellkampfgeschwader (SKG): 'fast bomber' (single-engined ground attack)

Zerstörergeschwader (ZG): 'destroyer' (twin-engined heavy fighter)

Various types of smaller autonomous units were similarly designated, e.g.:

Bordfliegergruppe (BdFlGr): shipborne floatplanes*

Ergänzungsgruppe (ErgGr): 'completion' (advanced training & replacement)

Erprobungsgruppe (ErpGr): trials (development & evaluation of own and enemy equipment)

Fernaufklärungsgruppe (F): long range reconnaissance

Küstfliegergruppe (KüFlGr): coastal aviation

Minensuchgruppe (MSGr): mine detection

Nachtschlachtgruppe (NSGr): night ground attack

Nahaufklärungsgruppe (H): short range reconnaissance, formerly: *Heeresaufklärungs* (Army reconnaissance), hence 'H'

Seeaufklärungsgruppe (SAGr): maritime reconnaissance

Jagdbomberstaffel (Jabo): fighter-bomber squadron within a JG

Luftbeobachtungsstaffel (LBeob): air observation

Seenotstaffel (See): maritime search & rescue

Wetterkundungsstaffel (Weku or Wekusta): meteorology

(* Luftwaffe and Kriegsmarine personnel worked together in mixed air and maintenance crews within these units.)

Aircraft Technical Personnel

In 1938 airfield ground crews became mobile Fliegerhorst-kompanien (air station companies) each attached to, and named after, an individual Geschwader. In late 1943 a redesignation gave each its own number. The precise number of assigned Fliegertechisches-Personal (aircraft technicians) varied widely according to aircraft type and quantity, with additional administrative staff provided by the host Luftgau.

Companies were divided into Züge, each of these platoons averaging 30 men under an Oberwerkmeister (line chief) and including airframe, engine and safety equipment fitters, armourers (ordnance and

May 1942: Oberst Adolf Galland arrives in Sicily to review operations against Malta, accompanied by the *Geschwaderkommodore* of JG 3 'Udet', Major Günther Lützow. Both wear continental service caps, tropical shirts and 'tropical assault trousers'.
Galland, former *Kommodore* of JG 26 'Schlageter', was appointed Inspector of Day Fighters at the age of 29 following the death in an accidental crash of his predecessor and friend Werner Mölders. Soon to be Germany's youngest general officer, Galland was a 'pilot's pilot', loyal to the regime but politically unre-flective. Although an essentially modest man, his outspoken campaigns against misappropriation, unreasonable demands, and the unjust accusations heaped upon pilots and ground crews by 'Fettig' ('Fatty') Göring often landed him in deep trouble, and after he was replaced by the politically reliable Gordon Gollob he came close to arrest by the Gestapo. The claim that Jagdflieger inflated their claims in order to qualify for the Knight's Cross so disgusted Galland that he removed his own decorations for almost a year. Galland was lucky to survive the war, which he ended as commander of the jet fighter unit Jagdverband 44; 'Franzl' Lützow was killed flying one of the unit's Me262s on 24 April 1945. (Private collection)

The highest scoring fighter ace in history: Hauptmann Erich 'Bubi' Hartmann of JG 52, pictured in Hungary in 1944, wearing a leather KW/41 jacket and beautifully 'softened' *Schirmmütze*; he would be one of only 27 German officers awarded the Knight's Cross with Oakleaves, Swords and Diamonds. (The Oakleaves and Swords were irreverently nicknamed *Kohl, Messer und Essbesteck* – 'cabbage, knife and fork'). Hartmann's Eastern Front total of 352 'kills', including 260 fighters, will surely never be matched.

The highest-scoring Allied aces are justly legendary – Ivan Kozhedub with 62 'kills'; Richard Bong with 40; and 'Johnnie' Johnson with 38 (all single-engined German fighters). Yet no less than 104 Jagdflieger were credited with more than 100 aerial victories, 35 with 150-plus, 15 with 200-plus, and two with more than 300 – and the Luftwaffe's criteria for crediting 'kills' were at least as rigorous as the Allies'. Such a staggering difference was largely due to two key factors.

The first was opportunity. The great majority of these *Abschussen* ('shoot-downs') were made on the Eastern Front, where the vast numbers of aircraft involved almost guaranteed potential targets on a daily basis. Initially, Soviet machines were slower and less well armed than German, and their pilots had far less training and experience. This was not the answer in itself, however: 20 German pilots were credited with more than 50 'kills', and ten with over 100, in combat solely against the Western Allies, where such conditions did not apply; furthermore, Erich Hartmann did not begin to gain spectacular results until July 1943, when the initial imbalance was long past, and new Soviet fighters had good low altitude performance.

The major factor was the accumulation and preservation of combat experience within the Geschwader. Unlike Allied pilots, who were entitled to a period out of the line after completing a set number of missions, the Jagdflieger remained operational (apart from perhaps two weeks' leave per year) until either their luck ran out or the war ended. They accounted for 70,000 of the 120,000 Allied aircraft destroyed during the war, but at a terrible cost: over 20,300 were killed, missing or wounded.

small arms), instrument and radio mechanics. These were supported by a Werkstattzug (workshop platoon) under a Zugführer, with engine fitters, sheet metal workers, painters, harness repairers, carpenters, electricians and technical storemen, many of whom were Zivilpersonal (employed civilians).

The airman of the Bodenpersonal (ground crews) was known by the nickname 'Schwarzemann' ('black man'), inspired by the overalls he wore in Spain, and soon shortened to the affectionate 'Schwarze' ('Blackie'). By the outbreak of war he was in fact just as likely to be dressed in off-white or dark blue, but the old name stuck. Many of these men were drawn from civil engineering backgrounds or had trained in aircraft factories, and a high proportion were career NCOs. Working round the clock with minimal sleep, these unsung heroes were invariably the first to rise and the last to turn in. They served in all conditions from desert sands to Arctic tundra, and had to endure minimal quarters and comforts; their devoted work seldom brought them any official recognition,

A rare unofficial snapshot showing *Luft-Nachrichten-personal* of an air-ground liaison team, with an Army Oberleutnant, during the operations in the West in summer 1940. Note the two main patterns of *Kraftfahrer-Schutzbrille* (vehicle driver's goggles). The truck mudguard apparently bears the oakleaf sign of 1.Panzer-Division above two 'Schwingen' – perhaps indicating use by a Luftwaffe Oberleutnant?

though they typically enjoyed a close relationship with their aircrew. Their lot was aggravated by the unrelenting demands to maintain a viable air force despite worsening shortages of everything, and they performed minor miracles on a daily basis to keep their machines airworthy.

Some groundcrewmen had previously failed aircrew training; others longed to avenge the loss of loved ones in a more direct way. Aircrew shortages on multi-seat squadrons gave them the opportunity to volunteer for specialist training as stand-in gunners and flight engineers, and several gained combat sorties to their credit.

Anti-aircraft artillery

The acronym 'Flak' is derived from Flug-abwehrartilleriekanone (flight defence artillery cannon), originally and correctly abbreviated to 'FlAK'.

Sharing the numeric designation of its parent Luftflotte, the largest formation was the Flakkorps comprising two or more Flakbrigaden or Flakdivisionen according to requirements. The brigade, designated by Roman numerals, normally comprised at least two Arabic-numbered Flakregimenter, plus signal, supply and air units.

While corps and brigade composition was flexible, that of the Flakregiment was fairly rigid, with an HQ staff and four Flakabteilungen (battalions) designated by Roman numerals (e.g., II./31 denoted II Abteilung of Flakregiment 31). First and second battalions were gun units, the third a searchlight (Höhenrichtkanone) unit, and the fourth a home-stationed Ersatz (replacement) training battalion. Abteilungen I, II and IV each contained three 'schwer' (heavy) and two 'leicht' (light) Flakbatterien. Heavy batteries usually consisted of 4x 8.8cm guns, one predictor and two truck-mounted 20mm mobile defence guns. Light batteries comprised 12x 20mm or 9x 37mm guns, and up to 16x 60cm search-lights. Batteries were numbered consecutively throughout the battalions: thus I Abteilung consisted of Batterien 1–5, II Abteilung of 6–10, III Abteilung of 11–13. The smallest operational unit was the Roman-numbered Flakzug (platoon), with two heavy guns served by 14–20 men, three medium guns by 24 men, or three light guns by 12 men.

The Flakartillerie was consistently the largest arm of the service; in 1939 almost two-thirds of total Luftwaffe strength of 1.5 million – over 900,000 men – wore the scarlet Waffenfarbe of the Flak. By autumn 1944, when the Luftwaffe peaked at 2.5 million, the Flak had expanded to account for over half of that total. Apart from those units deployed to combat zones, a deep concentration of guns was established to protect German cities and industry from the relentless Allied air offensive; and from 1944 Allied attacks on European airfields brought all Flak personnel firmly into the front line of combat.

Air Signals

This branch had a pre-war strength of c.100,000 men, and the composition of its elements was highly variable depending upon Luftflotte

August 1940: air gunners of a Channel coast Kampf-geschwader hone their skills with the 7.92mm MG15. The ordnance Waffenwart in the fore-ground, preparing fresh 75-round *Doppeltrommel 15* magazines, wears a well-worn example of the summer weight *Arbeitsschutzanzug 36*, now faded and washed to grey, and with a large repair patch to the sleeve.

Regular range practice was a vital part of an airman's life, and was often carried out in full flight gear to give it some realism. Until the mid-war years the defensive weapons were singly-mounted rifle-calibre machine guns, but later double mountings proved little more effective. In the Ju88 four machine guns were covered by the flight engineer alone; great agility was required to operate them all, including one rearward-facing mount in the ventral gondola. (Private collection)

July 1943: this ground crewman on a Focke-Wulf Fw 190A fighter squadron wears typical hot weather garb of grey-blue *Sporthose* and brown leather *Laufschuhe*. Before a mission he assists his pilot fasten his straw-yellow inflatable *Schwimmweste SWp 734*. The Jagdflieger wears a 1940 cream cotton jacket with shoulder boards, the grey-blue trousers of the K So/41 two-piece suit, and two-zip boots; note that red and white plastic pull-toggles have been added to the boot and jacket zips – a fairly common modification. The unit is unidentified; it might be JG 2 or JG 26 on the Channel coast; SKG 10 in Tunisia; or even I./JG 51 'Mölders', the first group to receive the Fw190A in Russia, in time to take part in the battle of Kursk – though a life vest would seem superfluous on the Russian steppes.

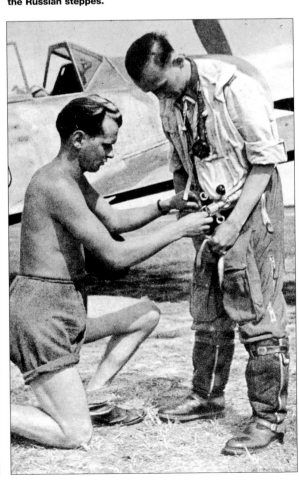

needs. Each fleet had three regiments (Luft-Nachrichtenregimenter) with anything from 1,500 to 9,000 personnel. The senior regiment shared the Flotte number, while the second and third added 10 and 20 to that figure respectively (e.g. Luftflotte 3 contained LN-Regimenter 3, 13 & 23). Each regiment was commanded by a Höhere Nachrichtenführer (higher signals leader) with the rank of Oberstleutnant, and consisted of three to five Luft-Nachrichtenabteilungen – including one Ersatzabteilung – a battalion being commanded by a Major and his staff of 40–50 officers and men. A battalion averaged three to four (or rarely, up to 20) Luft-Nachrichtenkompanien, each under a Hauptmann. Each was permanently attached to, commanded by, and named after a combat Geschwader e.g. LN-Kompanie KG 77. The company was divided into three to six Luft-Nachrichtenzüge, each specialising in a particular discipline: telephone, teletype, cable-laying, construction, radio, battery-charging, vehicle maintenance, radio- and light-beacon platoons. Each Züg contained between five and ten Luft-Nachrichtentruppen, the basic operational unit, each of 10 to 20 men.

Transport & Supply

Each Luftgau was assigned a Nachschubkompanie (supply company) comprising a Nachschubkolonnenstab (supply column staff), four Transportkolonnen (transport columns), and two or three Flugbetriebstoffkolonnen (aviation fuel columns). Companies had motor transport allotments of 50–100 vehicles, often supplemented with cars and trucks commandeered in occupied countries. Ground service and supply personnel had a combined pre-war strength of c.80,000 men.

Auxiliaries

From February 1942 the increasing demands on manpower prompted the formation of various auxiliary units, thus releasing men for front-line service. Helferinen (lit. 'female helpers') of the Luftnachrichten-Helferinenschaft (air signals women's auxiliary service) fulfilled mainly clerical and telephonic duties. Although not officially serving guns directly, Flakwaffenhelferinen operated Scheinwerffer (searchlight), Horchgeräten (sound detection) and Richtgeräten (altitude prediction) equipment in Flak units. Many received rudimentary instruction in gun crew tasks to enable them to give emergency assistance. Young male Flak-Helfer volunteers were drawn from the Hitler Youth, the RAD (Labour Service), and latterly direct from local schools. Over 75,000 schoolboys aged 15–16 operated Flak-Kanonen throughout Germany, their number bolstered by foreign volunteers and ex-POWs.

Fire Service

Established in 1935 from civilian fire service volunteers, the Fliegerhorst-Feuerwehr (air station fire defence, FhFw) was absorbed into the Luftwaffe in 1942. Service dress replaced their civilian uniform, but FhFw insignia were retained. A core staff of 14–18 men was established at each airfield with four to eight support personnel, assigned by daily roster, equipped and trained for fire-fighting. Although reclassified as Luftwaffemanschaften, they held Polizei status and were thus officially under the ultimate control of the Reichsführer-SS. In 1945 several Feuerwehrmänner equipped with Flammengewehre (flame-throwers) served as front-line assault teams during the battle for Berlin.

UNIFORMS & EQUIPMENT: SERVICE DRESS

Headgear

The **Schirmmütze** (peaked cap) had a grey-blue wool crown, black cotton band, and black leather or 'Vulcanfiber' peak. The enlisted ranks' model had a patent leather chinstrap, and crown and band piping in the wearer's Waffenfarbe (arm of service colour – see panel, page 16). Officers' caps carried plaited chin cords and piping in silver-coloured (or gold-coloured for generals) wire thread, irrespective of branch. Insignia consisted of the Hoheitsabzeichen der Luftwaffe (air force national insignia), a flying eagle clutching the swastika; this surmounted the Mützenabzeichen (cap badge), a Reichskokarde (cockade) in national colours supported by Eichenlaubkranz und Schwingen (oakleaf garland and stylised wings). Both insignia were of stamped white alloy for enlisted ranks, woven silver-coloured wire for officers up to Oberst, and gold-coloured wire for generals (see Plates A1 & C2).

The **Fliegermütze** (flyer's cap) was a simple grey-blue wool sidecap with a deep 'curtain' and rounded front and rear corners. A Hoheitsabzeichen, in white cotton thread for enlisted ranks and wire for officers, surmounted a slightly padded Reichskokarde woven onto grey-blue wool. Officers' Fliegermützen were further distinguished by wire or 'Celleon' (cellophane) piping to the edge of the curtain and the circumference of the cockade (see Plates A2 & G1).

From 19 December 1938, Luftwaffe Gebirgs Dienst (mountain service) units received a grey-blue **Bergmütze** (mountain cap) with a short peak, emulating the Austrian-style cap of Gebirgsjäger (mountain riflemen) alongside whom they served. Its deep folded curtain could be lowered to protect the neck and ears in cold weather, with the single-button flap closure fastened beneath the chin (see Plate G2).

On 11 June 1943, the Wehrmacht as a whole adopted the Einheitsfeldmütze 43 (M1943 universal field cap), itself inspired by the Bergmütze but with a longer peak and two-button flap closure. That issued to Luftwaffe personnel, the **Einheitsfliegermütze 43**, was of

The effective quad-mounted 20mm *Flakvierling 38* provides perimeter defence for an airfield in Russia, 1943; the crew's headgear consist of *Bergmützen* and a Red Army *ushanka* worn by the gun-layer. The Flakartillerie arsenal ranged from light 20mm automatic and medium 37mm pieces, to the heavy 88mm, 105mm and 128mm Kanonen, including twin-mounted Flakzwilling types. The Flakartillerie managed to inflict a great deal of damage, despite derisive claims about their effectiveness from some fighter pilots. There were at first some grounds for such scepticism; for example, in the West during August and September 1942 only five USAAF bombers were lost to ground fire, compared to 26 claimed by fighters. By the end of June 1944, however, that gap had closed to a 50 per cent differential, with cumulative totals of 886 lost to Flak and 1,682 to fighters. Moreover, in the same period the numbers of US bombers damaged by artillery and fighters stood at 21,459 and 3,290 respectively. In 1944–45 the heavy concentrations of light guns around Luftwaffe airfields in NW Europe also took a much greater toll on low-flying Allied fighters than did the Jagdflieger.

January 1939: an Oberfeldwebel assists ground crewmen in the transfer of an SC250 bomb from the hydraulic *Bomben-beladewagen* (bomb-loading trolley) into the *Einhängung* shackle of his Ju87A. The Stuka's 80-degree dive usually commenced from 15,000ft, reaching up to 350mph; coloured lines etched across the windshield helped the pilot assess his angle to the horizon. At 7,000ft – about 30 seconds into the dive – a horn sounded and the pilot pressed a control column button to initiate the bombing sequence. The automatic recovery system began to pull the aircraft out of its dive and simultaneously released the bomb shackle at 3,000ft. The bomb was swung away from the fuselage and clear of the propeller, slipping free in perfect continuation of the line of descent. The aircraft continued to draw itself back to level flight, thus covering for any temporary loss of consciousness from G-forces, until the pilot could resume control. A *'Stuka-Sirene'* was built into the undercarriage, generating its distinctive banshee wail; and *'Jericho Trompeten'* – compressed cardboard flutes emitting a high-pitched whistle – were fitted to the fins of many aerial bombs. These effects helped to shred the already shaken nerves of defenders who found themselves helpless under tactical air attack.

grey-blue wool with blue-painted alloy buttons (see Plate F1). Officers' Bergmützen and Einheitsfliegermützen bore wire piping to the crown seam only (see Plate H1).

Tunics

A grey-blue **Rock** or Tuchrock ('cloth tunic') with four pleated pockets, turn-back cuffs, exposed four-button front and open collar, was adopted for everyday wear early in 1935. The enlisted ranks' tunic had straight-edged pocket flaps, with patch breast pockets and expanding 'bellows' skirt pockets. It was lined in grey-blue cotton drill, incorporating an interior left breast pocket, Verbandstoff (wound dressing) pocket to the right front skirt, and short straps at the waist to accommodate belt-support hooks (see Plate C2).

Officers were obliged to purchase a fine quality equivalent for everyday wear, usually tailored in wool tricot cloth with sateen or cotton lining. All pockets were of patch type, with straight or gently scalloped flaps (see Plate A1). Generous turn-back cuffs routinely served as document pockets. A lightweight white cotton version, prescribed as Sommeranzug (summer dress), comprised Sommerrock, straight Sommer- or Weisse Hose (white trousers) and white-topped Sommermütze with removable crown for ease of cleaning (see Plate E3). Although officially suspended at the outbreak of war, its continued purchase was in fact permitted.

The most distinctive item of Luftwaffe dress, the **Fliegerbluse** (flyer's blouse), was developed concurrently for exclusive use as flying uniform. This short, close-fitting garment was simple and inexpensive to produce and quickly became the favoured tunic of all branches and on all occasions. The enlisted ranks' Fliegerbluse 35 was without external pockets and bore no national badge (breast eagle). Five large ceramic or fibre buttons were concealed by a fly front, and a convertible collar with a small hook-&-eye enabled it to be fully fastened

Selection – not exhaustive – of 'trade' badges for enlisted ranks. Machine-embroidered in light grey thread on grey-blue cloth discs approx. 5.3cm in diameter, they were worn on the left forearm of tunics. Silver-grey cord edging indicated NCOs in some categories, e.g. (7); in others, seniority in grade – e.g. (23). Badge (19) was awarded after nine months' service, but replaced by (25) from July 1937. Badge (22) was worn before qualification for metal aircrew badges – see Chart 3, page 44. *Equipment administrators:* (1) Admin NCO; (2) motor transport; (3) aircraft; (4) searchlight; (5) signals; (6) transport stores. *Qualified personnel & operators:* (7) Telephone; (8) teletype; (9) radio (10) sound locator; (11) direction finder; (12) radio instructor; (13) signals personnel in non-LN units; (14) medical personnel; (15) MT driver; (16) air warning service; (17) a/c radio mechanic; (18) armourer, Flak; (19) gun crew, Flak; (20) ordnance, aerial munitions – light; (21) aerial munitions – heavy; (22) aircrew; (23) flight technical personnel; (24) sound locator crew, Flak; with Gothic 'E' instead of 'H' = range finder crew; (25) gun crew, Flak; gold cord edging denoted one year's outstanding service or participation in destruction of enemy aircraft.

OPPOSITE **Flakartillerie Flieger Arnold Ortmann enlisted on 20 February 1943, yet his *Fliegerbluse 40* retains collar piping in arm-of-service colour, officially abolished from 20 March 1940. The removable *Kragenbinde* (collar band) could be worn with most types of tunic; each man was issued two of these grey-blue and white cotton linings, just 10mm of which was to be visible, providing some comfort and protecting the tunic collar from wear. The second pattern breast eagle, with up-swept tail, was adopted in 1936.**

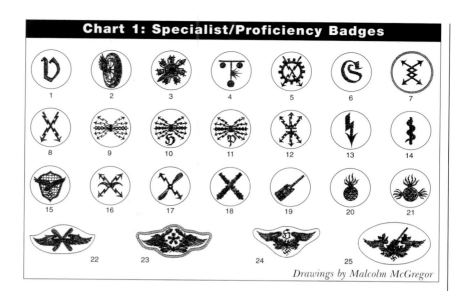

Chart 1: Specialist/Proficiency Badges

Drawings by Malcolm McGregor

at the neck when necessary. It was partially lined with grey-brown cotton cloth, incorporating buttoned interior breast pockets, belt-hook support straps, and buttoned field dressing pocket. The cuffs could be tightened; a small woollen tab stitched to the inside of the cuff could be passed through a slit in the rear seam to an external button, or alternatively it could remain secured to an internal button.

Officers' Fliegerblusen were essentially similar but of finer quality cloth and fully lined with sateen or cotton; as with most items of officers' kit, these privately purchased garments show many subtle variations in detail.

The upper part of the collars of both tunics bore edge-piping – Kragenlitze – in the appropriate Waffenfarbe for NCOs and enlisted ranks, silver for officers up to Oberst, and gold for generals. An order of 20 March 1940 discontinued the Waffenfarbe piping, but officers' bullion piping was retained.

From 6 May 1940 pockets were added to the skirts of the Fliegerbluse. These were internally hung but, for NCOs and enlisted men, had large external flaps with rounded corners, fastened with exposed alloy buttons; for officers they were gently curved and flapless.

An order dated 1 October 1940 stated that the national eagle badge was to be fitted to the right breast of the Fliegerbluse, reflecting the garments' elevation from work clothing to part of the Dienstanzug. Grey-blue 'Kunstseide' (rayon, synthetic silk) superseded cotton drill lining at the end of 1942, though the cut remained unaltered.

On 11 November 1938 a new dual-purpose tunic, the **Waffenrock**, had been approved as a replacement for both 1935 garments; this was identical to the Rock, except for a five-button front closure and convertible collar with concealed cloth tab and button ensuring a neat fit. The idea stood little chance against the popularity of the Fliegerbluse, however, and production ceased c.1940. A few Waffenröcke, usually privately tailored officers' examples, remained in use until 1945.

Insignia (for details see charts above & pages 17 & 44)

Model 1935 Schulterklappen (shoulder straps) displaying the appropriate Waffenfarbe were sewn into the shoulder seams of other ranks'

Röcke and Fliegerblusen 35. They were routinely manufactured from scrap cloth generated during tunic production. This fixed design, a feature common to most Wehrmacht uniforms, soon caused supply problems and so, on 20 March 1940, removable versions were adopted by all services. Often produced by home-workers, Schulterklappen 40 were supplied directly to issuing stores in the desired Waffenfarbe. Tunics were consequently manufactured with a cloth stirrup and button to each shoulder, also simplifying production. The use of fixed Schulterstücke (shoulder boards) continued on officers' Fliegerblusen and Röcke for smartness, although removable versions were available.

The status (i.e. officer, NCO or enlisted man), exact rank, and branch of service were identified on the collars of both tunics, with additional upper sleeve insignia for senior enlisted ranks. A special sequence of simplified upper sleeve rank patches were worn on flying clothing. Specialist qualifications for non-officer ranks were identified by badges on the lower (usually left) sleeve. Aircrew qualifications and accumulated mission awards were indicated by pin-on metal badges worn on the left breast. All the above will be found in Charts 1, 2 & 3.

Shirts & tie

NCOs and other enlisted ranks were to have no undershirt visible with either tunic or blouse, and a white V-necked pullover Trikothemd (tricot shirt) was supplied. For parade dress and special occasions, including their own weddings, a Weiss Hemd (white shirt) and Schwarz Halsbinde (black necktie) were permitted. Officers wore the cotton Blaumeliertes Hemd (mixed blue, i.e. blue mixed with unbleached thread) with separate button-on collar for everyday wear. They were to provide themselves with white shirts for best dress. Officially, a black tie was to be worn at all times.

On 27 September 1943 a grey-blue Stoffhemd (cloth shirt) was approved for wear without a tunic in hot weather by all ranks. These were provided with shoulder strap fittings, a machine-woven breast eagle on a triangular backing of matching cloth, and large, pleated breast pockets with buttoned flaps. A grey-green version, originally adopted from 17 December 1943 for field units, became standard issue to all ranks and branches on 19 September 1944 and the grey-blue type was discontinued.

Trousers

The straight grey-blue Tuchhose 35 issued to enlisted ranks incorporated slightly angled hip pockets, a buttoned slash pocket at the right rear, and a patch-type watch pocket to the right front; a rear V-notch and half-belt provided adjustment for the waistband. Some senior NCOs elected to wear Stiefelhose (breeches), with identical waist details. Officers' Tuchhosen and Stiefelhosen were of superior cloth and tailoring; pocket openings tended to be vertically set, buckled waist adjustment tabs were provided at each hip, and the watch pocket was internal. The popular Reithose (riding breeches) were identical to Stiefelhose but with the addition of inner thigh reinforcement panels in matching cloth or, more often, contrasting stone-grey suede or moleskin (see Plate A1).

Footwear

The traditional high Schaftstiefel (shafted boot), or the Schnürschuhe (laced shoe) adopted from 13 March 1941 for economic reasons, were worn by enlisted ranks. Officers wore soft black leather riding boots with breeches, and low-quarter black shoes with straight trousers.

Overcoat

A mid-calf length grey-blue wool Übermantel 35 completed the main uniform issue. The double-breasted coat had two rows of six standard Gekörnte-Knöpfe (pebbled finish buttons) to the front, slanted hip pockets with buttoned flaps, and turned-back cuffs. A rear half-belt provided adjustment and, when unfastened, allowed the deep-pleated coat to double as a blanket. Small metal hooks and thread loops permitted the skirts to be folded back to the hips, easing marching, but this was dropped during 1940, when the alloy buttons were also painted grey-blue. Shoulder straps and collar patches were worn on the overcoat, but the latter were officially abolished on 29 May 1942 (see Plate E1).

Fine quality officers' overcoats were usually lined with sateen cloth and, while details varied according to taste and budget, all were required to incorporate supports and access slit under the left pocket flap to attach the sword or dress dagger when appropriate.

The blanket-lined Einheitlicher-Tuchmantel (universal cloth overcoat) with enlarged collar, detachable hood and vertical hand-warmer torso pockets was approved on 17 October 1942.

WORK CLOTHING

The **Drillichmütze** (drill cap) was simply a black cotton drill version of the wool Fliegermütze, lined with black linen. It bore a dull white cotton national badge on black wool backing, but not the cockade.

The two-piece **Drillichanzug 35** (drill cloth suit) – styled the 'Drilchanzug' until 1940 – was originally issued in unbleached cotton, officially termed Rohgrau (raw grey); but from 16 July 1937 mechanics were to be supplied with a more practical black-dyed version. The unlined blouse was a fly-fronted, loose-fitting jacket fastening with four large ceramic or fibre buttons and one small dished alloy button at the neck; a hook-&-eye enabled the collar to be fully closed, and a cloth tab and button secured it when up-turned. The cuffs were split, adjustable to one of two dished alloy buttons. An internal left breast pocket replaced the original external patch type from 19 August 1936. The straight-cut drill trousers had buttoned flaps to the hip pockets, and a buttoned slash pocket was added to the right rear from 19 August 1936. Alloy friction buckles with cloth straps were provided at each side for adjustment, and small slits below the waistband could be secured over Taillenhaken (belt support hooks) fitted to the blouse. Economy dictated a return to Rohgrau drill cloth from 4 June 1940, although the Drillichmütze remained black. The blouse was often tucked into the trousers, giving the impression of a one-piece overall, and black and undyed items were frequently worn in combination (see Plate F1).

In addition to the more popular Drillichanzug, one-piece overalls were also available in both lined and unlined versions. The **Arbeitsschutzanzug 36** (working protective suit), approved 4 April 1936, was again originally issued in Rohgrau cotton drill, but from July 1937 these too were supplied in dark blue or black. A front fly closure was fastened with eight buttons, the upper five being of the large type found on the Drillichbluse, and the lower three of smaller size; there were also a hook-&-eye and a buttoning cloth tab to the collar. Hip pockets let into the side seams were coupled with access slits to clothing worn under the suit. Adjustment to cuffs was by cloth straps and buttons, and to ankles by tie-tapes. A matching cloth waist belt with an alloy friction buckle passed through narrow loops at each hip, and an open-topped, centrally divided patch pocket was fitted to the left breast (see Plate B1). In 1937 a second type appeared, with the breast pocket enlarged and moved to the right side, the dividing stitch-line deleted, and a large buttoned flap added. The waist belt, prone to snagging on parts of the aircraft, was replaced by internal cloth tunnels containing fixed cotton tie-tapes.

The 'Arbeitsschutzanzug, gefüttert' (lined) matched the unlined suit in style, colours and modifications, but was produced in heavier denim of tight herringbone weave; body and legs were lined with blanket cloth, and the sleeves, crotch and seat had cotton reinforcements – this suit weighed approximately 6lbs (see Plate G1).

These suits remained largely unaltered throughout the war, although from late 1942 the cotton parts of the lined overalls were being replaced

---

OPPOSITE **Chart 2: Rank Insignia**
Each numbered block shows *Kragenspiegel* collar patch; *Schulterklappe* shoulder strap (1-10) or *Schulterstucke* shoulder board (11-20); *Winkel* chevron for service uniforms (2-5), or special rank insignia for flight clothing (6-20). Prior to 20 March 1940, all enlisted ranks wore *Waffenfarbe* cord to tunic and blouse collars. Officers' collars and collar patches were edged with silver cord, and general officers' with gold cord.
COMPONENTS:
ENLISTED RANKS (1-10), collar patch of appropriate *Waffenfarbe*; silver-grey alloy *Metallschwingen* insignia; blue-grey cloth shoulder strap with *Waffenfarbe* piping. NCOs (6-10), silver-grey lace collar & shoulder strap *Tresse*; (8-10) silver-grey alloy *Sterne* stars. OFFICERS (11-16), *Waffenfarbe* collar patch; silver wire *Schwingen* wings, & *Eichenblätter* oakleaves (11-13) or *Eichenlaubkranz* garland (14-16); silver wire board with *Waffenfarbe* underlay; gilt metal stars (12-16). GENERAL OFFICERS (17-20), white collar patch; gold wire wings, eagle, oak garland; gold/silver/gold shoulderboard on white underlay; gilt metal stars.
Chevrons (2-5) worn on left upper sleeve, silver-grey lace & embroidered star (5) on blue-grey cloth. Special rank insignia for flight clothing (6-20) introduced both sleeves 24 December 1935, left sleeve only from 4 August 1942. *Doppleschwingen, Stern & Querstreifen* crossbar (6-16) white, (17-19) gold-yellow, (20) gold wire, all on cloth or leather backing approximating colour of clothing.
RANKS:
ENLISTED MEN: (1) Flieger; (2) Gefreiter; (3) Obergefreiter; (4) Hauptgefreiter; (5) Stabsgefreiter. NCOs: (6) Unteroffizier; (7) Unterfeldwebel; (8) Feldwebel; (9) Oberfeldwebel; (10) Stabsfeldwebel. OFFICERS: (11) Leutnant; (12) Oberleutnant; (13) Hauptmann; (14) Major; (15) Oberstleutnant; (16) Oberst. GENERAL OFFICERS: (17) Generalmajor; (18) Generalleutnant; (19) General der Flieger, Artillerie, etc.; (20) Generaloberst.
NOTES: (4) = cancelled 12 May 1944; (5) introduced 4 February 1944; (7) = also Fähnrich, junior officer candidate, denoted only by silver Portepee bayonet-knot; (9) also Oberfähnrich, senior officer candidate, with silver cord piping to collar in place of NCO Tresse.

WAFFENFARBEN:
AA Artillery - Hochrot (bright red); Air Signals = Hellbraun (light brown); Transport & Supply = as per branch to which attached; Pioneer = Schwarz (black); Flight, air & ground = Goldgelb (gold-yellow); Medical = Dunkelblau (dark blue); Airfield Security = Hellgrun (light green).

Drawings by Malcolm McGregor

with rayon. Large stocks of military overalls and work clothing were appropriated from occupied countries, and supplies of these frequently augmented the German models. Occasionally 'Blackie' was able to acquire worn-out items of flight clothing from aircrew to make his life a little more comfortable. Particular favourites were flight boots for warmth on cold, wet airfields; and the trousers of the two-piece flight suit, with all their useful pockets for tools and spares.

Insignia were sparse, but junior ranks could wear the Winkel (chevrons) appropriate to their grade on the left sleeve. NCOs were distinguished by a full-length (or from 4 September 1942, partial) Kragentresse to the collar (see Plate F1). A system of Ärmelstreifen (sleeve stripes, worn around the cuffs) was adopted from 27 May 1935 for senior NCOs: Feldwebel was denoted by a single stripe, Oberfeldwebel by two, and Stabsfeldwebel by three and a stylised star. The breast eagle was seldom worn on work clothing.

The wearing of steel-studded **boots** when working around fuel- and ammunition-laden aircraft carries the risks of sparks, slipping, and damage to the thin alloy skin of the aircraft; nevertheless, the majority of maintenance personnel routinely wore them. Some removed the studs, while others – at their own or unit expense – had replacement rubber soles fitted. Large Gummiüberschuhe (rubber overshoes), fastened with four (or, from 1938, two) steel clips, were a limited issue until materiel shortages cancelled them in c.1941. Many elected to wear rubber-soled canvas sports shoes. In the main, thin rubber or padded canvas mats were draped across wing roots to provide safe purchase and protect the aircraft.

This Flak Gefreiter, pictured in 1940, sports the rolled shoulder straps which were very occasionally seen during the French campaign. Simply formed by turning the strap back on itself and securing with a few stitches, this modification prevented rifle and equipment straps from slipping off the shoulder. Clearly inspired by the French practice, it was also occasionally seen on the overcoat. Note on his forearm the gunners' specialist qualification insignia adopted on 23 July 1937, denoting a minimum of nine months' service.

RIGHT **An Oberfähnrich (NCO serving as a probationary officer) displays a fine example of the Schirmmütze unique to this rank: officers' aluminium wire chin cords are fitted to an enlisted ranks' cap with Waffenfarbe piping to band and crown. His use of woven cap insignia was officially only permitted when off-duty. Silver Litze has been added to the collar patches and collar edge, and a press-stud between the lower two buttons prevents unsightly gape in the absence of a belt, further enhancing the appearance of his privately tailored Rock. The national badge is set extremely low on he pocket flap.**

FLIGHT CLOTHING

Flight helmets

Flieger-Kopfhauben were produced in both summer and winter weights, either with or without integral Funk-Telegraphie/Telephonie or FT-Gerät (radio-telegraphy/telephony equipment). Throat microphones were fixed to a leather neck strap attached to the nape of the helmet, with press-stud fastening at the front. The internal communications loom emerged just above this in a 1.3 metre long cable with a black plastic quick-release jack plug. Oxygen mask fittings comprised flat metal hooks at the sides, and an adjustable wire stirrup mounted inside a tunnel at the crown. A pair of press stud-fastened leather straps to the rear sides secured the headband of the goggles. The helmets incorporated an awkwardly over-complex system of twin chinstraps, one having to be passed through a slit in the other.

Principal summer-weight helmets were the Flieger-Kopfhaube für Sommer mit FT-Gerät – Baumuster S 100 (flight helmet for summer with RT equipment, Model S 100), and the LKp S 101; both made of Braunmeliert (mixed brown) thread Schilfleinen (reed linen), lined with tan or grey 'Kettatlas' sateen. Winter-weight versions, of dark brown leather with lambswool lining, were designated LKp W 100 and LKp W 101. The 100-series were identifiable by domed black-lacquered aluminium earphone covers (see Plates A3 & B2). The 101-series, adopted c.1938, featured improved communications equipment and leather-covered plastic earphone covers, incorporating a small ridge which held the goggle headband in place (see Plates B3 & C1).

A lightweight version, the Flieger-Netzkopfhaube or LKp N 101, with fine-mesh crown for improved ventilation in summer or the tropics, was approved on 16 June 1941 for use by fighter and destroyer pilots, but soon found favour among other aircrews. The earphones were set within large rigid leather side panels, connected by leather bands across forehead and nape. Oxygen mask fixing hooks were augmented or replaced by hexagonal-based aluminium posts fitted to the leading edges of these side panels, creating two distinct models. The first could take all two- or three-strap mask types, while the other (without adjustable crown stirrup) could only accept two-strap masks.

The communications cable had always been

something of an encumbrance and was frequently shortened by base technicians, sometimes drastically so, with the balance transposed to the aircraft interior fittings (see Plates E3 & F3).

One-piece flight suits

Most of the world's air force flying suits were simple developments of conventional overalls, with little consideration given to their potential as an aid to survival; their wearers continued to rely upon the chance of recovering survival packs stowed in the aircraft itself. Although the Fliegerschutzanzug (flight protective suit) was officially designated simply as a Kombination (overall), successive models incorporated innovative features that later became standard in flight clothing design the world over.

Fliegerschutzanzüge were available in summer and winter weights, further sub-designated for flight over land or sea, the latter constructed of materials affording greater insulation. Most aircrews followed this system of matching suit to environment, although availability or personal preferences often dictated what was worn.

Summer: Developed from the K So/33 of the DLV, the Kombination, Sommer, 1934 (K So/34) was made of the same lightweight, durable Braunmeliert cloth as the LKp S helmets. The most notable feature was a long, concealed zip-fastener running diagonally from left hip to right shoulder, where it was covered by a buttoned wind-flap. A zipped patch pocket for maps, etc. was set high on the left breast. A vertically mounted 13.5cm x 3cm brown leather strap, stitched to lower mid chest and forming two separate loops, provided anchorage for the oxygen mask hose clamp. The sleeves were of three-piece 'raglan' style, incorporating elasticated inner cuff bands with zip closures to the cuff proper. Zip-fastened openings were provided at each hip for access to trouser pockets beneath, and horizontally zipped internal pockets to each knee accommodated survival equipment. Inner calf seams also closed with zips, and the crotch was fitted with a horizontal fly (for easier opening when seated). The K So/34 underwent a series of minor changes, creating seven principal variations.

On 17 December 1935 the addition of a short press-stud strap to each sleeve cuff was ordered, to prevent the zip fastener creeping open.

The adoption of an inflatable Schwimmweste (life jacket) in 1937 triggered the most significant development. It was intended that the suit be worn *over* the vest to protect it from snagging in the aircraft and chafing by parachute harness; it was therefore necessary to provide quick access to the vest's inflation canister. The most immediate solution was the insertion of a short zip at the midriff, just below and parallel to the main zip (see Plate A2). When the vest required oral topping-up, however, the collar and main zip would have to be unfastened in order to reach its inflation tube.

The Berlin company of Karl Heisler developed a quick-opening 'Reissverschluss' (rip-fastener) device, comprising a series of 35 leather loops passed through 36 steel eyelets and secured by a cord.[1] Tied to the centre of the cord, and concealed beneath a triangular safety flap with press-stud fastening, was a large steel Griffring ('grasp ring'); a

---

1 A similar device, with 13 loops secured by a leather cord, was used on Heisler's padded Flieger-Knieschutzer knee-protectors, also available to airmen.

This Obergefreiter wears a grade-6 *Schiessauszeichnung* (marksmanship lanyard), SA-Wehrabzeichen, and belt buckle correctly aligned with the edge of the tunic. The more sartorially inclined airmen found many ways to enhance this already smart uniform for *Ausgehanzug* (walking-out dress). The *Fliegerbluse* could be retailored and even shortened, sometimes drastically so, rendering the pockets almost useless. Its somewhat fractured lining created many geometric patterns to the front panels and, when a replacement could be obtained, great care was taken to select the garment with the palest, most visible stitching. *Tuchhose* would be soaked in warm water, with wooden boards forced into each leg, and then left to dry. The desired silhouette was a close-fitting jacket and baggy trousers. (Martin J.Brayley)

Ground crew on a Heinkel He45C unit wear grey-blue *Fliegermützen* and the two-piece *Drillichanzug* in black. The *Taillenhaken* (belt support hooks) fitted to the blouse could be secured through a slit at each side of the trouser waistband, just visible on the two men at left. Note the full length collar *Tresse* of the senior NCO at second right.

Cockpit of a Heinkel He111, pictured c.1941. The *'Spaten'* ('spade' – from the shape of the tail fin) had been able to out-run fighters over Spain, but was already nearing obsolescence by 1940; nevertheless, shortages of more modern types kept it in production until late 1944. The observer (left), here wearing a KW Fl bR/40 suit, LKp W 100 helmet (and, unusually, a small beard), served as navigator, bombardier, air-gunner and, occasionally, co-pilot. Many aircrew received informal instruction from their pilots, which might give them a chance of taking over the controls in an emergency. The pilot favours the K So/34 suit and LKp W 101 helmet, with twin throat micro-phones clearly visible. A narrow flip-up windshield in the cockpit roof, and a telescopic seat, afforded him a slightly better view – albeit an uncomfortable one – when taxying at night or in bad weather. (Martin J.Brayley)

continuous pull on this drew the cord from its tunnel and opened the fastener.

This design gave complete and rapid access to both the vest's inflation canister and the mouth tube. The large opening also provided for the expansion of the vest and alleviated chest restriction. Its presence dictated the omission of the chest pocket (see Plate A3). Heisler exclusively supplied the device to contracted flight suit manufacturers, hence the appearance of Karl Heisler labels (stitched directly to the fastener) inside suits made by Cunsel & Schroedter of Berlin, Bekleidungsfabrik Habett of Württemberg, and Striegel & Wagner ('Striwa') of Bavaria. To speed production, Friedrich Emmerich of Berlin and Tschache & Co of Dresden later made the device under licence. The rip-fasteners were delivered with cord ends knotted to prevent accidental deployment, and many appear to have remained that way throughout their service life.

From 20 May 1937 manufacturers were instructed to fit zipped pockets into the outer thigh seams for two wound dressing packets (at left), and the Flieger-Kappmesser 37 (aircrew knife) secured within a small inner pocket; a width increase from 47mm to 50mm to this inner pocket was ordered on 10 November (see Plate A3). Finally, on 7 June 1940, a slightly reduced left breast pocket was reinstated, now internally mounted with zipless external access. The fly zip was simultaneously lengthened and set vertically. As if in recognition of aircrews' persistence in wearing the suit under rather than over the life vest, oxygen hose chest loop-straps were reduced to 2cm wide and positioned slightly higher – encroaching on the pocket – to avoid obstruction by the vest (see Plate B2).

Winter, Land: The Kombination, Winter, Land, 1933 (KW l/33) – nicknamed the 'Bayerisch' (Bavarian) – was of fine quality grey-blue or

brown 'Velveton' moleskin cloth, lined throughout with sheepskin. A conventional vertical front closure was retained, in keeping with its contemporary K So/33 and KW s/33, but fastened with eight large ceramic buttons rather than a zip. Large patch pockets with deeply scalloped flaps and ceramic buttons were provided at the hips and just above the knees. These suits generally lacked the chest loop-straps of other models, the oxygen hose being clipped to the front placket instead. Despite its designation, possible use for flights over water prompted the addition of a vertical Schwimmweste access zip to the right of the button closure, or the Heisler-Reissverschluss. Outer thigh knife and dressing pockets also appeared concurrently with those of the summer model (see Plate G2).

This layout remained unaltered until 7 June 1940, when all future production was ordered standardised with other types. The button front was replaced by a diagonal main zip, a vertical fly was added, and an internal pocket with external access was fitted to the left breast – existing stocks could be modified with an external patch pocket.

Winter, Sea: Evolved from the leather KW s/33, the KW s/34 was made of dark brown 'Kalbin' (calfskin), with diagonal main zip, heavy fleece lining, and large black or brown mouton collar. Principal details and modifications followed those of the K So/34 although, during 1940, the bulky hide was rejected in favour of supple 'Nacktpelz' (lit. 'naked pelt', or sheepskin); the suede outer surface was left undyed. The KW s/34 was fitted with midriff zip or Heisler-Reissverschluss from 1937, sometimes concurrently. Although the zip could be resealed, thereby preserving some warmth and comfort when immersed, it was difficult to operate with cold, wet or gloved hands.

The KW s/34 was costly and slow to produce, and a pre-war Austrian type, distinguished by two full-length zips running from collar to ankle cuff, was frequently issued instead.

Electrically heated: When necessary, winter suits could be worn over the dark grey cotton Kombination mit electrischer Beheizung (K 20/24) – an electrically heated undersuit adopted from 25 June 1936. This was worn in conjunction with Flieger-Füsslinge mit electrischer Beheizung (F 20/24) heated socks, and Flieger-Handschuhe mit electrischer Beheizung (Ha 14/24) heated gloves, worn over fine Unter ziehwoll-handschuhe (lit. 'under heated wool gloves'). The power cable of the heated clothing left the suit at the small of the back, and could be passed through a hip pocket vent of the outer suit for connection to the aircraft's circuit. This suit fell from use by 1939.

For single-seaters: The winter suits, awkward enough in the confines of a bomber, were quite unsuitable for the tiny cockpit of the Bf109, although many saw such use. On 16 February 1940 a new Kombination, Winter, für Flugzeuge mit beschränkten Raumverhältnissen, 1940 (KW Fl bR/40 ?) was approved for use in 'aircraft with limited space'. These comparatively lightweight suits, of tightly woven grey-blue 'Schappe' synthetic silk twill, were lined throughout with 4mm Schappe velveteen

Kanalkampf 1940: Beobachter Feldwebel in the nose of a Heinkel of I./KG 4 'General Wever', based at Soesterberg, Holland. He wears the K So/34 suit with special sleeve rank insignia, and LKp S 100 helmet. Just visible are the *Schnellklinkhaken* (quick-latch hooks) to the front of the *Brustfallschirm* harness, to which the parachute pack was rapidly attached when required. The large fully-glazed nose of the He111, with its off-centre MG15 mount, gave little protection from shell fragments; it also had a tendency to distort the pilot's view and reflect sunlight back into the cockpit. (Hans Obert)

The medium bomber crew comprised the Flugzeugführer (pilot), Beobachter (observer), Bordfunker (radio operator), Bordmechanik (flight engineer) and Bordschutz (gunner) – most of them in fact doubling as gunners when all guns were manned simultaneously. Most of the crew were stationed together in the nose sections of their comparatively small He111s, Do17s and Ju88s; consequently, well-placed enemy fire could rapidly inflict devastating casualties.

of deep blue or purple, which also faced the large fall collar. Although not heated, the suit bore an electrical circuit with external connectors at wrist and calf, to convey power from the aircraft's rheostat supply to heated gloves and boots (see Plate B3). Of standard diagonal-zipped style with Heisler-Reissverschluss, this suit was also subject to the modifications of 7 June 1940.

Two-piece flight suits

Production of one-piece suits was officially halted on 24 April 1941, although some existing contracts were not completed until 1942. Each type was henceforth to be produced as a Flieger-schutzanzug, Kombination (zweiteilig) 1941, and these two-piece suits began to see service by the middle of that year.

The jacket was a relatively simple affair with single left breast pocket, and a double loop-strap of leather or matching cloth to one side of the vertical main zip. The real advance lay in the design of the trousers, with their voluminous pockets for rescue and survival equipment. The selection of items carried was to individual choice, but routinely included emergency rations and medical kit. Frequently worn with jackets other than that intended, the trousers offered not only versatility and greater ease of movement, but had obvious practical advantages during latrine visits... The use of insignia on the two-piece suits was limited; breast eagles and sleeve rank badges or epaulettes were often fitted to the cloth versions, while sheepskin types were usually left unadorned.

Summer: The jacket of the K So/41 had a small fall collar with press-stud tab, and plain split cuffs with two-button adjustment. The bulk of production was in grey-blue (sometimes grey-green) cloth with wool-knit waistband, but an alternative version was produced in the same tan Braunmeliert cloth as its parent K So/34. This type had a matching cloth waistband, adjustable at each side by internally mounted alloy friction buckles and cloth straps, and closed with two 'Prym' press-studs. Stocks of the tan cloth were exhausted during 1943. The trouser waistband was adjustable by friction buckles at each hip front, and fitted with buttons or web loop attachments for cloth braces. An internal flannel apron was often fitted to prevent heavy equipment from chafing the wearers' thighs (see Plates D2 & F2).

Winter, Land: The KW l/41, equivalent of the 'Bayerisch' KW l/33, was primarily manufactured in soft blue cloth (occasionally olive-green), with sheepskin lining and large fleece collar. The canvas waistband had friction buckle adjusters. In addition to an internal chest pocket with external opening, two diagonal slash pockets were set at lower front and usually fastened with press-stud tabs (see Plate F3). Trouser cloth tended to be more tightly woven than that used for the jacket and of a deeper grey-blue colour.

Winter, Sea: Original production of the KW s/41 was of high quality natural sheepskin with dark brown or black inner fleece and collar. The single patch chest pocket and loop-strap were either of matching suede or contrasting leather, and the canvas waistband fastened with two press-studs. Diagonal slash pockets with press-stud fasteners were later added. The sheepskin trousers were considered too weak to support fully laden survival equipment pockets and so lacked this feature. Canvas reinforcement panels extending from the waistband were incorporated to distribute the load and resolve this weakness, these versions being produced in brown and grey-blue dyed sheepskin with similarly coloured pockets and reinforcements (see Plate C3).

Electrically heated: The KW Fl bR/41 was of the same heavy duty grey-blue canvas as the one-piece KW Fl bR/40, with Schappe lining and connectors for heated boots and gloves; similar contacts were necessarily added to the waistbands of jacket and trousers to complete the circuit (see Plate F3). An all-leather version of this suit was produced in late 1943, of substantial black, brown or grey hide, to provide limited protection from the highly corrosive synthetic fuels then in use (see Plate H3).

Non-issue flight jackets

Jagdflieger were quick to adopt practical items suited to the close confines of the cockpit, a short leather jacket being the preference. Such garments were not issued but generally purchased at individual expense from various sources, and some sub-units or just small groups of friends would acquire matching jackets. Among the most coveted of the home-produced versions was an expensive black leather suit with distinctive zip-fastened slash pockets (see Plate H1). With the occupation of conquered nations countless alternatives were readily available from civilian outlets wherever the pilot was stationed. Differences in cut, fastenings and

The KW l/33 'Bayerisch' winter suit in its original form. The double-button cuffs and the knee pockets are clearly visible on this light brown example, as are the collar fastening straps. The buttoned front incorporated a double flap for effective insulation. His other equipment consists of the LKp S 100 helmet, and partially fastened *Sitzfallschirm 30-l* seat parachute with snap-hook fittings rather than the later *Schloss-Autoflug* buckle. (Martin J.Brayley)

Sicily, early 1941: a Messerschmitt Bf110 crewman of ZG 26 'Horst Wessel' examines the M1891/24 carbine of an Italian airfield guard. The Unteroffizier wears the electrically wired KW Fl bR/40 suit with synthetic fur collar; a connector for the heated gloves can be clearly seen on the forearm, and the *Doppelschwinge* of his rank is on summer-weight *braunmeliert* cloth backing. The kapok *Schwimmweste 10-76A* is the original full-backed version with lifting collar.

The Bf110 'destroyer' proved during the Battle of Britain to have no credible future as an unescorted heavy fighter, and was consistently outfought by single-engined types. On fronts where such opposition was rare – Africa and Russia in 1941 – it briefly remained useful as a light reconnaissance bomber; and it was later successfully converted for night interception, with a third crewman to operate the airborne radar. (Private collection)

pockets soon proliferated, with a particular French style among the most popular. The occasionally encountered cloth versions tended to be blue, grey-blue or cream, with wool-knit waistband, collar and (sometimes) cuffs. When fitted with insignia the flight jackets were extremely handsome in appearance – which naturally appealed to the inherent panache of fighter pilots. Although collar patches were rarely added, a few NCOs applied *Metallschwingen* directly to the collar.

Additional sources were the British Air Ministry, US Army Quartermaster Department and Soviet *Voiyeno-Vozdushnui Syl* – many items being 'souvenired' from downed Allied aircrews. The USAAF A2 flyers' jacket was a particular favourite (see Plate E3), and was routinely worn by the legendary Heinz Bär; while Adolf Galland was famously pictured in RAF Irvin sheepskin jacket and trousers. Whatever their origin, all were for operational wear only and were not permitted to be worn off-base, where a more 'military' form of attire was demanded.

Gloves

Four types of brown leather Flieger-Lederhandschuhe were adopted in 1933. Summer types were designated 'mit' or 'ohne' Stulpe, Ungefüttert ('with' or 'without gauntlet, unlined'), HS 5 m/33 and o/33. Winter equivalents were designated 'gefüttert' (lined), FW 5 m/33 and FW 5 o/33. Press-stud or buckle-fastened straps were provided at wrist and cuff for a wind-resistant fit. Electrically heated FW m/40 gloves developed for the wired KW Fl bR/40 and /41 suits were of soft grey-blue or brown suede, with 8w/24v element, fine Schappe lining, and connectors at the gauntlet cuff. Black, brown and grey-blue coloured heated and unheated gloves were produced in conjunction with the all-leather KW/41 suit.

Footwear

The Flieger-Pelzstiefel (flyer's fur-lined boots) had a stout leather foot with rubber heel and sole. The black or charcoal-grey sheepskin shafts had full-length steel zips at inner and outer calf, to ease fitting over several layers of clothing; the outer calf zip was discontinued for economy during 1940. Leather tightening straps, buckled around the top of the shafts and across the front of the ankles, were intended to prevent boots being torn off by parachute opening shock. Material quality deteriorated from the mid-war period, with shafts assembled from joined off-cuts rather than single panels, and fugitive dyes resulted in some discoloration; but construction standards remained high. Heizbare Flieger-Pelzstiefel (heated flyers' boots) for the KW Fl bR/40 and /41 suits differed only in the inclusion of an 11w/24v electric element inside the lining and leather connector tabs at the outer top.

High quality brown leather and suede boots with inner calf zips, commercially available from Paul Hoffmann & Co., Berlin, were particularly popular during the early years (see Plate A2). Black all-leather Flieger-Überziehlpelzstiefel (lit. 'over heated fur boots') with fine white

(continued on page 33)

BLITZKRIEG, 1939–40
1: Oberstleutnant, LN-Regt 24; Vienna, September 1939
2: Major, KG zbV 1; Western Front, May 1940
3: Feldwebel, 3./StG 2 'Immelmann'; Britain, August 1940

NORTH-WEST EUROPE, 1941-42
1: Obergefreiter, III./KG 40; France, summer 1941
2: Stabsfeldwebel, I./KG 51 'Edelweiss'; France, March 1941
3: Oberleutnant, Seenotstaffel 10; Norway, 1944

B

C

NORTH AFRICA & MEDITERRANEAN, 1941–43
1: Flieger, Flak-Regiment 33; Libya, 1941
2: Leutnant, 2./(H)14; Libya, May 1942
3: Unterfeldwebel, 1./(F)122; Sardinia, February 1943

NORTH AFRICA & MEDITERRANEAN, 1942–44
1: Feldwebel, Pioneer-Kompanie, JG 27; North Africa, autumn 1942
2: Gefreiter, Ersatzbataillon XI; Libya, 1942
3: Leutnant, 5./JG 4; Italy, 1944

E

NORTHERN EUROPE, 1942–44
1: Unteroffizier, 2./KG 200; Berlin, summer 1944
2: Oberleutnant, Erg-ZGr; Poland, summer 1942
3: Fähnrich, II./ZG 76; East Prussia, autumn 1944

F

EASTERN FRONT, 1943–45
1: Flieger, 3./KG zbV 1; Stalingrad, winter 1942/43
2: Oberfeldwebel, II./SG 2; Hungary, December 1944
3: Stabsgefreiter, Flakartillerie airfield defence, Romania, January 1945

DEFENCE OF THE REICH, 1944–45
1: Hauptmann, 12./NJG 1; Holland, January 1944
2: Oberhelferin, 14.Flakdivision; Germany, October 1944
3: Oberfahnrich, III./KG 76; Germany, March 1945

1

2

3

H

lambswool lining, designed for wear over the electrically-heated F 20/24 socks, were officially discontinued in June 1939 but remained in (vigorously polished) service throughout the war.

SAFETY EQUIPMENT & SURVIVAL AIDS

Headgear

Aircrew seeking increased head protection initially had to improvise with the standard issue Stahlhelm 35 or 40, some of which had the sides forced or hammered outward in base workshops so as to accommodate the earphones of flight helmets worn underneath. Several experimental models followed from 1940 – e.g. the Flieger-Sturzhelm (crash helmet), and Siemens SSK 90 constructed from leather-covered steel plates – but trials proved unsuccessful. A Flieger-Stahlhelm proper, similar in design to the Fallschirmjäger style but with large cut-outs for the earphones, was finally adopted in late 1944, but was produced in very limited numbers and saw little use.

Oxygen masks

Numerous models of Höhenatemmaske were employed. Most comprised a green rubber facepiece, sometimes with a soft leather skirt for warmth and wind protection, and were secured to the helmet by two or three elastic or sprung straps. The hose was ribbed to prevent twisting or icing. The most common models were the HM 5 or HM 15 (large) and 10-67, with three-strap fittings; the two-strap 10-6701, occasionally converted to three straps; the three-strap 10-6702, and the two-strap 10-69. These were variously produced by Auer-Gessellschaft of Berlin, and Drägerwerke of Lübeck.

Goggles

Late 1930s developments culminated in the M295 and M295a Windschutzbrille (wind protective glasses) with one-piece grey-brown rubber frame; and the M306 Fliegerschutzbrille with separate rubber eyepads connected by a screw-adjusted bridge. The curved lenses permitted optimum vision, while offering good protection from flying debris. Most were supplied by Auer or Lietz, in a metal or cardboard container complete with cleaning leather or cloth and a selection of 'Neophan' or 'Umbral' tinted lenses against solar, searchlight or snow glare. Splitterschutz-

May 1942: *Ritterkreuzträger* Hauptmann Kaminski (left), of JG 53 'Pik As', receives a typically animated explanation of a mission over Malta, at the height of the air campaign which briefly neutralised British offensive air and sea operations from the island. The Luftwaffe theatre commander Gen. Kesselring urged an immediate Italo-German airborne invasion (Operation 'Hercules'), which is unlikely to have failed, but Hitler refused – transport and supply shortages, apparent successes in Africa, and memories of the heavy casualties in Crete were all contributory factors.

Kaminski's cream cotton jacket with grey-blue wool waistband and collar with twin press-stud closure was particularly popular in Russia and the Mediterranean. It was approved from 4 July 1940, but production was cut short by the introduction of the *Flieger-schutzanzug (zweiteilig)* in 1941. (Private collection)

brille (splinter protective glasses), with non-refractive lenses developed by Nitsche & Günther, consolidated all these attributes.

Life vests

Aircrew serving in single-seat and multi-seat aircraft could wear either of two main types according to preference or availability.

The first was the Heisler-designed kapok-filled Schwimmweste 10-76A, of dull yellow cotton canvas and distinctive semi-rigid 'sausage' construction, with cord

loop and wooden toggle fastenings, and a large lifting collar designed to hold the wearer's head above water. The design quickly proved a danger to unconscious or wounded airmen: as the back panel was larger than the front, and therefore more buoyant, it could easily flip a man face-down in rough water. Introduced by the end of 1940, the improved SW 10-76 B1 overcame the problem by replacing this panel with a simple yoke and system of web straps. At the same time the collar was slightly remodelled and fitted with a set of snap-fastened chin supports (see Plate B3).

The second, more compact type was the inflatable Schwimmweste pneumatisch 734 10-30 (SWp 734) developed by Drägerwerke in 1936–37. This was made of soft proofed cotton duck, and activated by means of a 0.06 litre compressed air cylinder mounted on the lower left front panel, or a rubber mouth inflation tube on the left breast. The SWp 734 had a brown-coloured body with contrasting brick-red shoulder yoke and collar section, and fastened with grey-black webbing straps and double O-ring friction buckles at waist and mid-chest. Although some aircrew wore the inflatable vest in the prescribed manner, under the flight suit, the great majority did not. It was a practical step, therefore, to replace the dull brown with a more visible yellow colour to assist in rescue operations, but the vest remained otherwise unchanged (see Plates A3 & B2).

The SWp 743 suffered from a design fault similar to the kapok-filled type, in that its back panel incorporated an inflation bladder below shoulder level, causing the same danger of inversion. A simultaneous redesign resulted in the SWp 743 10-30 B1 with open back, yoke and strap arrangement. Early 1941 saw the introduction of the 10-30 B2, differing only in the replacement of some metal fittings with cheaper plastic – in particular the nickel-plated mouthpiece to the inflation tube, which in extreme cold could freeze to a man's lips (see Plates E3 & F3).

Parachutes

Like most contemporary air forces, the Luftwaffe employed three distinctive configurations of parachute; adopted in 1936, these remained

Channel coast of France, 1943: Fw190A-4 fighter-bomber pilots of SKG 10. From October 1940, Bf109E-7s fitted with racks for a single SC250 bomb, to carry out Jagdbomber raids on British targets, were issued to single Staffeln within the Jagd-geschwader. The fighter pilots hated the drag on their speed and manoeuvrability, and initial efforts were half-hearted. Allocation of more important targets, and their own escort, lifted morale, and the 'Jabo' pilots developed pride in their accuracy. The task was turned over to new Schnell-Kampf-geschwader in spring 1943 when the two Channel fighter wings, JG 2 and 26, could no longer afford this distraction from their interceptor role.

The Oberleutnant and Major wear finely tailored examples of the officers' *Fliegerbluse*, while the Hauptmann, Leutnant and Feldwebel wear the grey-blue K So/41 two-piece flight suit, with sleeve insignia mounted on dark blue cloth, and SWp 10-30 B2 life-vests. Single-seater pilots generally favoured the inflatable vest for convenience in their cramped cockpits, but even minor damage to the air chambers could render it useless. (Hans Obert)

essentially unaltered until 1945. The principal models in wartime use were the seat-type Sitzfallschirm 30-IS-24B (fl 30231); back-type Rückenfallschirm 12B (fl 30245); and Fallschirm-gurt 30-II-24 (fl 30208) harness with quick-attach Brustfallschirm 10-3 D1 (fl 30210) chest pack. Selection was dictated by aircraft type and crew position; the aircrew of single- and two-seat aircraft using back or seat types, while the different members of bomber crews needed all three.

All contained an average 7.32m diameter canopy (5m when deployed) of white silk or 'Mako' synthetic weave; this could be safely deployed at speeds of up to 400km/h (250mph), giving an average descent rate of 6.5 metres per second. Much pre-war development had been shared between Germany and Great Britain and all three models bore striking resemblances to their RAF counterparts, not least in the use of the quick-release Schloss-Autoflug (SA) buckle copied from the British Irvin design (see Plates B2, B3 & G2). Like Allied types, but unlike the Fallschirmjäger pattern, the harness featured webbing risers from the shoulders which kept the centre of gravity high for a safer landing.

Russia, winter 1942/43: an Oberfeldwebel pilot and his Feldwebel wireless operator – wearing the Luftwaffe *Bergmütze* – of a Ju52 unit. Both men wear the *Front-flugspange für Transport und Luftlandflieger* above Iron Cross 2nd Class and *Ostmedaille* ribbons, and pin-backed Iron Crosses 1st Class. The 'Oberfeld' also wears the *Deutsches Reichsabzeichen für Leibesübungen* (DRL) sports badge, instituted in 1937 for maintaining high levels of physical fitness for 12 months. Transverse braid on his shoulder straps denotes *Offizieranwärter* (officer aspirant) status.

The huge distances and primitive infrastructure of the Eastern Front put great demands on the transport fleet, which provided vital resupply and evacuation bridges to various encircled 'pockets', but their numbers were quite inadequate to save the 6th Army at Stalingrad.

The Russian winter caused almost as many accidental aircraft losses as those incurred in combat. During the first winter only about 25 per cent of all machines were serviceable at any time.

Additional equipment

A broad range of survival equipment was provided for aircrews, dictated by environment. This included highly nutritious Absprungverpflegung ('bail-out subsistence' rations), Model 9 'Esbit-Kocher' folding field cookers with solid fuel tablets, Sanitätspack (medical kits), quilted kapok-filled Schlafsack (sleeping bags), and high quality machetes.

Two-, three- or four-man Rettungschlauchbootes (inflatable rescue dinghies) could be stowed in larger aircraft, or an individual Ein-mannschlauchboot was carried in a special pack on the man himself. The battery-powered NSG1 Funkgerät (radio transmitter) originally stowed with these boats was superseded, from 1941, by the smaller generator-powered NSG2 & 4 models; these hand-cranked versions offered far greater duration, with the added benefits of keeping men active, focused and warm. Recognition equipment included the Farbbeutel (dye-marker pouch), Sichtfahne (signal flag) and Rauchsichtzeichen (smoke marker).

A decorated Feldwebel fighter pilot in Russia wearing the sheepskin KW s/41; this combines undyed trousers, without knee pockets, and a grey-blue jacket – both items had canvas waistbands with friction buckle adjusters. He also wears a single-button *Bergmütze*, and a *Schlupfjacke 42* cardigan under his *Fliegerbluse.* His awards are the *Frontflugspange für Jagd-flieger* and Iron Cross 2nd and 1st Class, and below the latter he wears his pilot's qualification badge – *Flugzeugführer-abzeichen* – with a black Wound Badge barely visible beside it.

Mid-1944: a wide assortment of winter and summer flight gear can be seen in this III./JG 3 line-up. Occasionally encountered modifications to the K So/41 suit included the addition of large pockets to the jacket, and sup-porting buttons to the centre of each knee pocket flap, and base personnel have here added pull-tags to the flaps. Early use over British waters gave rise to the now famous sobriquet 'Kanal-hosen' (Channel trousers), a term probably more popular today than during the war. Unusually, the man second from left has fixed the Ärmband-kompass to his boot strap. Pulled back from Russia in August 1943 to boost the home defence force, III./JG 3 was led by Walther Dahl, who would end the war as the joint leading ace against Allied four-engined day bombers.

Crewmen routinely carried a Leuchtpistole (flare pistol) with a generous supply of coloured Signalpatrone and Leuchtpatrone (signal and flare cartridges), along with Fallschirmsig-nalpatrone and Fall-schirmleuchtpatrone 41 parachute types. The initial practice of carrying cartridges loose in a pocket was unsatisfactory. Various commercially produced Taille-Riemen für Leucht-patronen (waist straps for flare cartridges) saw limited use but were awkward to wear with the parachute and life vest (see Plate F2). By far the most practical method was the ten-round Patronengurt worn round one or both lower legs.

The gravity-activated Flieger-Kappmesser 37 knife was primarily to enable bailed-out airmen to cut themselves free of entangled parachute risers and shroud-lines. Some standard flight equipment, such as the Ärmbandkompass 39 (wrist compass) and Luft-Navigationskarte (air navigation maps), could be equally useful on the ground. The durable plasticised-linen maps were often printed

July 1943: a Ju88 observer offers his pilot a biscuit during an 11-hour high-altitude recon-naissance flight over central Russia. Both wear Auer 10-67 oxygen masks with three-strap fitting clearly displayed. A large A-clamp at the base of the hose secured it to the chest loop-strap of the Kombination, to prevent fouling of flight controls. Both wear the LKp W 101 helmet, but in an interesting contrast, the pilot favours second type *Splitterschutzbrille* goggles and K So/41 suit, while the observer chooses the KW Fl bR/40 or /41 suit with FW m/40 gloves and civilian prescription spectacles.

on yellow background cloth that gave a clear, less reflective image under red night-lights.

TROPICAL UNIFORM

By comparison with colonial powers, Germany had had only limited experience of such uniform before the war. In 1940 well-established foreign designs provided the starting point for the Hanover Institute's Tropical Studies Department, and the resulting uniforms were among the best in the Wehrmacht's inventory – practical, comfortable, versatile, and dashingly modern in appearance.

While those of the Army tended toward an olive green hue (see Plate D1), Luftwaffe Tropenanzug was of more traditional orange-sand colour – at least when new. The combined ravages of African sun, dust storms, heavy sweating and frequent washing (often in petrol, marginally less scarce than water) all took their toll, and some items became bleached almost white. Resupply problems kept heavily worn and repaired items in use longer than was normally acceptable. Shirts and footwear suffered most, although these could occasionally be supplemented from captured Allied stocks. Apart from insignia, the items constituting Tropenanzug 41, issued to all ranks and branches, were identical from Flieger to General.

Headgear

The cloth-covered **Tropenhelm** (sun helmet) had a noticeably deep curve to the wide brim, providing efficient protection, and a tan leather chinstrap. It was usually lined with light green, a combination of tan and green, or occasionally orange cotton cloth; these colours, like the red of the Army version, were believed to provide the best defence from solar radiation while allowing body heat to dissipate. Stamped metal insignia, following those worn on the steel helmet, were fixed to each side of the Tropenhelm in the form of a Wappen (shield) of national colours to the right, and the Luftwaffe's flying eagle Hoheitsabzeichen to the left.

Far more popular was the **Tropenfliegermütze** (tropical flyer's cap), a lightweight cotton version of the wool Fliegermütze, usually lined with fine tan linen. The cap bore a dull white eagle woven onto tan cotton backing, but retained the continental Reichskokarde. Period photographs and surviving examples regularly show a vertical crease to the centre of the body, having been folded and carried in a pocket when not required.

All ranks were also entitled to the **Tropenschirmmütze mit Neckenschutze** (tropical peaked cap with neck protector). These heavy tan cotton caps had a broad crown, a distinctly large peak and a button-on neck curtain which gave good protection, but were costly to produce and difficult to store and carry. They were supplied with

BeVo[2] woven versions of standard Schirmmütze insignia; but some officers chose to embellish them with wire or metal equivalents, added crown-seam piping, or bullion wire chin cords substituted for the original ½in. brown leather chinstrap (see Plate D2).

Strangely, the Luftwaffe did not issue its own official version of the famous **'Afrikamütze'**, although some factory-made examples were available, and some personnel had approximations made up by unit or local tailors. These caps are often slightly less shapely than the official Army pattern (e.g. without the small bulge to the crown front), and generally lack ventilation eyelets to the sides. Another expedient was simply to add Luftwaffe insignia to a traded or 'liberated' Army issue cap.

Pilot and wireless operator/ air gunner of a Ju87B-2 congratulate each other on a successful mission, providing a good view of the *Sitzfallschirm* seat parachute harness and flight helmet communications cable. A standard three-colour Diamon field torch is attached to the WOp/AG's belt, just visible below the parachute release handle. Both wear high-laced boots remarkably similar to the paratroopers' *Fallschirm-schützenstiefel 41*. The 'E87' on a yellow triangle, next to each of the aircraft's filler points, refers to the octane rating of the dark blue-coloured B4 grade aviation fuel. (Martin J.Brayley)

Tunic

The **Tropenrock** (tropical tunic) was a four-pocket design with convertible collar, echoing the failed Waffenrock 38, but with six-button closure and made of hard-wearing cotton canvas. The collar fastened with a single hook-&-eye and a concealed tab and button, although this was rarely used. A tropical Hoheitsabzeichen, heavily woven in dull white on a tan backing, was machined above the right breast with tight zigzag stitching during manufacture. Only the breast pockets were pleated, while skirt pockets were of 'bellows' construction; some of the more frugal manufacturers cut the main panel in two sections and joined them with a central vertical seam. The shallow cuffs had buttoned vents allowing some adjustment. Only the armpits and pockets were lined, with a combination of heavy canvas and absorbent open-weave hessian, although belt hook support straps and field dressing pocket were retained.

Shirts and tie

Both the **Tropenhemd 'mit lang'** and **'mit kurz' Ärmel** (tropical shirts with long and short sleeves) were of robust cotton and featured fashionably long, pointed collars which could accept plastic stiffeners. Large pleated breast pockets had deeply scalloped flaps. A special version of the breast eagle, woven in white onto a triangular cotton backing ranging in hue from tan to light chocolate, was provided, as were cloth stirrups and brown-painted pebbled alloy buttons for the Schulterklappen 40. The front and pocket buttons were of either brown or grey ceramic, composition fibre or dished steel, and most were removable by means of a smaller plastic button sewn to the rear. Both types of shirt featured very long tails enabling them to double as nightwear, and spare cloth was often cut from these to repair worn collar and cuffs. For walking-out and parade dress the broad cotton **khakibraun Tropenbinder** (tropical necktie) was worn.

---

2 Acronym from Beteiligung-Vorstehre, the developing manufacturer of this finely machine-woven style of insignia.

Spring 1941: Unteroffizier Schubert poses with his Bf109E-4 of 3./JG 1 at De Koj, Holland. Before issue of the two-piece flight suit items like this flare pistol had to be secured wherever possible – usually tucked into a boot or, as here, tied to the life vest. Despite its awkward bulk the kapok SW 10-76 B1 was favoured by some fighter pilots for its warmth, superior float-duration, and ability to sustain even a sizeable tear with little effect upon buoyancy. The flat cap worn by the central ground crewman distinguishes him as a civilian technician; the mechanic at right wears non-standard, perhaps foreign-made overalls with two breast pockets. (Hans Obert)

OPPOSITE A group of bomber crewmen, wearing a mixture of kapok-filled and inflatable life vests, undergo gruelling survival training aboard a two- to four-man dinghy. Their instructor (left) wears the original brown-coloured version of the SWp 734, displaying its problematic back section. Note immediately behind him the large compressed air cylinder for rapid inflation of the dinghy, lashed at the bow. Extra equipment stowed in the craft included three-section alloy oars, top-up bellows (visible here), and a yellow-green flourescine dye *Farbbeutel.*

Trousers

The long **Tropenhose** were of conventional straight cut. They featured a matching cloth waist belt with an alloy friction buckle, contained within a tunnel, two rear pockets with gently scalloped concealed-button flaps, and two angled slash hip pockets. They saw only limited service, production being halted during 1942 in favour of the more comfortable and practical **Tropen-überfallhose** (lit. 'assault trousers'). These had very loosely cut legs, with a large map pocket to the front of the left thigh, and were gathered and bloused at the ankle by means of a strap and buckle arrangement like that of the waist belt. This could be fastened in two ways: either through the buckle, or (more quickly) drawn across the front of the ankle and engaged with a small button at the outer seam. One manufacturing variant used narrow square-ended straps fastening to machine-stamped, open-frame steel buckles like those found on Gebirgsjäger Rucksacke and Gelkenbinden (puttees) (see Plate E2).

Kurz Tropenhose (tropical shorts) followed exactly the line of the trousers, terminating just above the knee. In the Wehrmacht the wearing of shorts was officially restricted to off-duty periods, other than walking-out, in rear areas only. In North Africa their use on front line bases was permitted, and shorts were even occasionally worn as flight clothing.

Some officers and senior NCOs chose to wear tropical versions of the **riding breeches** produced in tan whipcord fabric (also occasionally used in the manufacture of the Tropenrock, Tropenhose and Überfallhose), but these were unpopular due to the discomfort of tightly fitted calves.

Footwear

Throughout the first half of the desert campaign most personnel had to wear the standard issue long or ankle boots; unless regularly oiled the leather was prone to severe cracking from the harsh, dry heat, particularly at the toe-bend and ankle. During 1942 the specially developed ankle-high **Tropen-Schnürschuhe** and higher **Tropen-Schnürstiefel mit Segeltuchschaft khakibraun** ('with khaki-brown canvas shaft') began to arrive in quantity (see Plates E1& E3).

Overcoat

Unlike the Heer, the Luftwaffe did not adopt a tropical version of the overcoat, and the grey-blue Übermantel remained standard despite the extreme cold of the desert nights (see Plate E1).

WINTER UNIFORM

Headgear

Apart from the issue sheepskin **Pelzmütze** with short peak and curtain (see Plate C3), a wide variety of headgear from various sources was employed. Some were fashioned by the men themselves, who occasionally inflicted unofficial modifications upon the standard Fliegermütze in the

'Afrikaner' Friedrich Knoppe from Brandenburg, early 1943. The *Tropenhelm*, shirt with special triangular-backed breast eagle, and the integral waist belt of the *Tropenüberfallhose* are all visible. The canvas uppers to Luftwaffe tropical boots were usually tan in colour, rather than the greener shades of Heer issue.

BELOW **A Flak unit truck driver on the Eastern Front is almost swallowed whole by his full length sheepskin coat. Generally fastened with wooden toggles or horn buttons to cord or tape loops, they gave good protection for those in exposed or static positions.** *Pelzmützen* **fleece caps were fitted with cap- or tunic-sized** *Hoheitsabzeichen*. **Many tons of civilian clothing items – occasionally completely inappropriate in design and colour – were donated during 'Winterhilfs' (winter aid) drives in 1941 and 1942; scarves, hats, gloves, sweaters and waistcoats of all descriptions were distributed, and welcomed. (Lee Attwells)**

form of rabbitskin or sheepskin curtains to the sides. Some acquired the high-topped Romanian lambswool *caciula*, or the Red Army *ushanka* with folding earflaps.

Undergarments

Supplementary **Angorawäsche** (angora wool underwear) was issued, and some were lucky enough to receive a 37–42cm by 120–150cm flannel **Leibbinde** (waistband), a traditional item which helped maintain body core temperature. Two types of grey-white ribbed-knit sweater, with 15mm grey-blue collar stripe, were available. The six-button cardigan-style **Unterjacke** had a V-neck designed to be unseen when worn with the Rock or Fliegerbluse. The round-necked pullover **Schlupfjacke 36** had a three-button placket that could be turned back out of sight when necessary. The collar stripe was omitted on the replacement Schlupf-jacke 42. Quilted rayon **Zwischenweste u. Zwischen-hose** (lit. 'between-vest & between-trousers'), fastening with cotton tapes, were produced from 1941, the trousers with external waistband loops through which braces were passed before buttoning to Tuchhose. Although intended as additional inner layers these items were occasionally worn as outer garments. Sheepskin waistcoats and rabbitskin jackets, **Pelzjacke**, with large axial vents for ease of movement, were also produced as undergarments but frequently worn as topcoats (see Plate G3). The grey knit **Halschal** (neck scarf) and **Kopfschützer** (head protector) – a tubular toque – provided additional insulation.

Overgarments

Full length sheepskin coats with cloth collar and tape-reinforced seams were issued to personnel in exposed positions, such as vehicle drivers and gunners. Thigh-length versions with a large fleece collar were also produced. Late in 1941 uniquely styled cotton canvas oversuits were developed, reversible from olive-grey to white and with distinctive squared or diagonally-stitched quilting, but these were mainly issued to Fallschirmjäger. This extravagance was dropped during mid-1942 in favour of the Army's **schwere Winteranzug** (heavy winter suit), comprising Überziehjacke, Überziehhose, Kopfhaube or Kappe (hood)

and Fausthandschuhe (mittens). The mouse-grey, and later Buntfarbendruck (mixed-colour print) and Sumpfmuster (marsh pattern) camouflaged sides were either fully reversible to Altweiss (off-white – see Plate G3), or non-reversible with grey-blue rayon lining. Huge stocks of captured or salvaged Soviet quilted jackets and trousers were washed, repaired and re-issued.

Footwear

The enormous **Filzschuhe** (felt shoe) adopted from 5 March 1940, and often wrongly described as unpaired, were designed to fit over standard boots during prolonged static duties – particularly sentry duty. Coarse hair felt uppers, buckled at front or rear with two leather straps, were stitched to rigid leather toe and heel sections, which in turn were nailed to thick wooden soles to distance and insulate the feet from snow and ice (see Plate G1). An alternative type was available to those engaged in more active tasks, such as vehicle and artillery crews. Stout grey hair-felt uppers with brown leather front and rear seam reinforcement were stitched to a leather foot, or often separate heel and toe sections, with moulded rubber soles (see Plate G3). A similar third type, **Schneestiefel** (snow boots), chiefly used by motorcyclists and drivers, had proofed and lined white canvas uppers and shafts, incorporating lace-up collars that could be drawn to form a wind- and snow-tight seal below the knee. Whitened leather reinforcing strips overlapped the noticeably peaked toe section. Soviet *valenkii* felt over-boots also saw widespread use.

North Africa, Christmas 1942: preparing bread in a 'kitchen' fashioned from egg crates, these Bäkereikompanie cooks wear an array of sweaters – from left to right, *Schlupfjacke 36*, and civilian roll-neck, sleeveless, and V-neck. The headgear includes bazaar-made *'Afrikamützen'*, and (second right) an issue *Troppenschirmmütze*. This cap acquired the slang name 'Hermann Meyer', in reference to a nickname for Göring; like him, it was said to be 'large, well ornamented, and not of much practical use'.

SELECT BIBLIOGRAPHY

Angolia, John & Adolf Schlicht, original documents quoted in *Uniforms & Traditions of the Luftwaffe,* vols I–III (California, 1996–98)
Argyle, Christopher, *Chronology of World War II,* (London, 1980)
McGuirk, Dal, *Rommel's Army in Africa,* (London, 1987)
Price, Alfred, numerous titles
Shvanyebakh, B.E., *Rukovodstvo po Nemyetskomu Voennomu Perevodu,* (Moscow, 1943)
Tschoeltsch, Generalmajor Ehrenfried, *Der Dienst-Unterricht in der Luftwaffe,* (Berlin, 1941)
British War Office & US War Department publications, various.

LEFT **Grey-blue and olive-grey versions of the *Tropenhelm, Tropenrock, lang & kurz Tropenhose, Tropen-Schnürschuhe* and *Tropen-Schnürstiefel* (though apparently not the *Tropenfliegermütze* or *Überfallhose*) were produced for service in hot but non-desert climates, and were common in the southern Russian and Italian theatres. Photographed near Stalingrad in summer 1942, this Feldwebel from JG 77 wears the grey-blue version of the *Tropenrock*.**

THE PLATES

A: BLITZKRIEG, 1939–40

A1: Oberstleutnant, Luft-Nachrichtenregiment 24; Vienna, September 1939

The 'Höhere Nafü' of LN-Regt 24, a signals unit of Luftflotte 4, wears the standard officers' Schirmmütze and Rock – although many favoured more useful 'bellows' skirt pockets in the style of the enlisted ranks' tunic. Pinned to his right breast is the Spanish Cross without swords, signifying a non-combatant veteran of the Legion Condor. The white and black ribbon of the Iron Cross marks his Great War service. The service belt and P38 holster are in the russet leather distinctive of the Luftwaffe.

A2: Major, Kampfgeschwader zbV 1; Western Front, May 1940

This Ju52 pilot, preparing to transport paratroops of 9./Fallschirmjäger Regt 1 from Gütersloh-Rehda airfield to their drop zone in Holland, wears the 1937 version of the K So/34 flight suit with diagonal life vest access zip at the midriff. The series of special sleeve rank insignia for flight clothing, comprising wings and bars, were introduced at the turn of 1935/36. His flare pistol is tucked into his boot, with cartridges carried loose in a knee pocket, and a Walther P38 automatic – unusually – protrudes from the zipped chest pocket. His Fliegermütze bears the standard officer's distinction of silver piping to the curtain edge. The brown flying boots are of the type made by Hoffmann of Berlin.

A3: Feldwebel, 3 Staffel/Stukageschwader 2 'Immelmann'; Battle of Britain, 16 August 1940

Returning from a raid on an RAF fighter airfield, this wireless operator/air gunner's Ju87B-2 was forced down near Selsey, Sussex. He removes his SWp 734 10-30 life vest, here of transitional manufacture with grey web front straps, revealing details of a rarely seen version of the K So/34 suit with Heisler-Reissverschluss and horizontal fly zip. At his feet lie his discarded LKp S 100 helmet and M295 goggles. See page 38 for seat parachute details.

While most downed aircrew were quickly rounded up by Local Defence Volunteers, police or service personnel, some unfortunates fell into the hands of British housewives armed with kitchen knives and fire-pokers before they could be rescued by the authorities; a few of the more savage beatings proved fatal.

B: NORTH-WEST EUROPE, 1941–42

B1: Obergefreiter, III Gruppe/Kampfgeschwader 40; Bordeaux-Mérignac, France, summer 1941

This Bombenwart (ordnance armourer) wears the M1935 drill cap, and first pattern unlined black one-piece Arbeitsschutzanzug, illustrating belt, cuff and pocket details, and the double Winkel of his rank on the left sleeve. The central dividing seam was often removed to produce a more practical breast pocket. He has rubber overboots, and has acquired HS 5 o/33 gloves. Note the cardboard tail-fin flutes fitted to the Spreng Cylindrische SC50 (high explosive, general purpose 50kg) bomb. Other principal types included the Spreng Dickwand (high explosive, thick-walled) and Panzerbombe Cylindrische (armour-piercing, general purpose) – in weights of 50kg (110lb), 250kg (550lb), 500kg (1100lb) and 1000kg (1 ton); largest of all was the SC3500 ($3\frac{1}{2}$ ton) 'Max'. KG 40 operated the Do217 and Fw200 'Condor' on anti-shipping duties across the South Atlantic.

B2: Stabsfeldwebel, I Gruppe/Kampfgeschwader 51 'Edelweiss'; Melun-Villaroche, France, March 1941

Preparing for an early evening raid over Portsmouth naval dockyard, this Ju88A-1 flight engineer dons a typical assortment of summer and winter clothing. He wears M306 goggles over the sheepskin-lined LKp W 100 helmet, with fitted high-visibility cover in case of 'ditching'. The communications cable is tucked into the chest pocket, and an Auer HM 15 oxygen mask hangs from the chest loops of his final pattern K So/34 suit. The leg cuffs are fastened over his boots in an effort to secure them during parachute opening shock. At his feet are FW 5 m/33 gloves, the back-type parachute pack, and his 734 10-30 life vest. He hopes that the steel helmet with lining removed will provide protection against AA shell splinters.

B3: Oberleutnant, Seenotstaffel 10; Tromso, Norway, 1942

After a successful rescue off Nordkinnhalvoya on the Barents Sea, this Do24 floatplane observer enjoys a coffee even before removing his chest-type parachute harness and kapok 10-76 B1 life vest, with dye-marker pack attached. Auer M295 goggles are worn over the LKp W 101 helmet. Note the connectors of the electrically wired KW Fl bR/40 suit for heated boots and gloves (dropped onto the navigation equipment case). Sea rescue crews of both sides routinely took pity on each others' ditched aircrews, and would notify their enemy counterparts of the location via Swiss shipping radio. Rescue aircraft were originally painted white with large red crosses, but received camouflaging colours during 1941 after several were shot down by the Royal Navy – due to their habit of reporting Allied convoys to the Kriegsmarine.

The double silver braid sleeve stripes worn by this Pionier Oberfeldwebel denote his temporary appointment to Hauptfeldwebel (first sergeant), commonly known as 'Der Spiess'. Broadly equivalent to 'philistine', this slang term is difficult to translate succinctly, but alludes to someone who shouts a lot. These insignia of appointment, not rank, should not be confused with rank distinctions for work and protective clothing, upon which the Spiess would wear three white sleeve stripes. The 'WL' vehicle registration prefix is abbreviated from Wehrmacht-Luftwaffe.

C: RUSSIA & HOME FRONT, 1941–43

C1: Hauptmann, III/Jagdgeschwader 77; Sarabus, Crimea, September 1941

This Bf109F pilot wears uniform typical of the first summer in the USSR. Over Blaumeliertes Hemd and black tie, he sports a commercially acquired leather jacket of French origin; a metal clip at the waistband was more common than a button. Thread loops fitted to the chest accommodated pin-backed awards to avoid piercing the jacket itself, although the awards have been temporarily removed to prevent damaging the life vest. Note matching angles to hip and watch pockets of his finely tailored Stiefelhose. Uniform breeches and trousers were still de rigeur at this date, but the new two-piece Kombination and Tropenüberfallhose became widespread during 1942. The LKp N 101 helmet is worn here with second type Nitsche & Günther splinterproof goggles with elastic strap; the orange-tinted lenses effectively reduced glare. Standard officer's belt with holstered P08, and single-zip boots, complete his attire.

C2: Hauptgefreiter, Sanitätskompanie; North Compound 3, Stalag Luft 1, Barth, spring 1943

Checking the contents of a Red Cross parcel, this POW camp medic favours the Schirmmütze and Rock, here with dark blue medical Waffenfarbe, although from 1940 these were mainly kept for parade or best dress. Braid loops to the epaulettes mark him as an Unteroffizieranwärter (NCO aspirant). He wears the medical specialist badge on his left forearm, the Eastern Winter 1941/42 medal ribbon in the upper buttonhole, and a black Wound Badge. Situated near the town of Barth in Pomerania on the Baltic coast, Stalag Luft 1 was opened in October 1942 and liberated by the Red Army on 1 May 1945; it held around 9,000 Allied airmen, mostly USAAF, in four compounds.

C3: Unteroffizier, Kampfgruppe zbV 172; Demjansk airlift, Russia, February 1942

Overseeing the balanced loading of his 'Tante Ju', this transport crewman is protected by the issue Winterpelzmütze, civilian fur-backed ski mittens, and brown sheepskin KW s/41 suit. Most of the latter were produced in occupied Eastern territories, this example by Knebl & Ditrich of Indija, Croatia. Extreme weather conditions caused endless mechanical problems, but only the very worst prevented take-off. Between February and May the transport units delivered 24,000 tons of supplies to the 100,000 troops trapped in the Demyansk Pocket, as well as airlifting in a further 15,446 men and evacuating 20,093 casualties. The operation cost 262 Ju52s and 385 men, including this unit's Kommandeur, Major Walter Hammer.

D: NORTH AFRICA & MEDITERRANEAN, 1941–43

D1: Flieger, 1 Batterie/Flak-Regiment 33; Libya, 1941

Among the first Luftwaffe units to arrive in Libya with the Afrikakorps were Flak-Regimenter 6, 18 & 33. Keen to distinguish themselves from Army personnel, these men soon modified their Army-issue Tropenanzug 40 by adding Luftwaffe distinctions – most commonly the red collar patches – although most retained the Heer version of the breast eagle. The red-piped shoulder straps and Tropenmütze required no alteration, although some replaced the cap badge with its Luftwaffe equivalent. This gunner

Hauptmann Bruno Stolle, *Gruppenkommandeur* III./JG 2 (July 1943–February 1944), wears one of 13 commemorative cuff bands bestowed upon distinguished units from 1935. The 33mm blue wool bands were embroidered in Gothic script – here 'Jagdgeschwader Richthofen' for JG 2 – in aluminium wire or grey-white thread. The other bands awarded to flight units were 'Jagdgeschwader Schlageter' (JG 26); 'Gesch-wader Horst Wessel' (ZG 26); 'Geschwader Immelmann' (StG 2); 'Geschwader Hindenburg' (KG 1); 'Geschwader General Wever' (KG 4); 'Geschwader Boelcke' (KG 27); 'Legion Condor' (KG 53); and 'Tannenberg' (NAGr/(H)10). The 1941 War Order of the German Cross, worn on his right pocket, was awarded in silver for repeated outstanding service or in gold for combat exploits deserving more than the Iron Cross 1st Class but not warranting the *Ritterkreuz*. JG 2 and JG 26, known to Allied airmen as 'the Abbeville boys', were the main 'Kanal Geschwadern' charged with defending the French and Belgian coasts between 1941 and 1944.

wears a re-issued French Mle 1935 shirt with button-down collar. The Luftwaffe Tropenanzug (Plate E2) replaced this uniform during the following year, but many veterans mixed old Heer items with new Luftwaffe issue. He carries a Munitionskasten (ammunition case) containing two 20-round magazines for the 20mm Flak-38 Kanone, with hand-applied dark yellow paint over the factory-sprayed field-grey.

Chart 3: Aircrew Qualification Badges & Mission Clasps

1 2 3 4

5 6 7

8 9 10

Drawings by Malcolm McGregor

Aircrew badges (Fliegerabzeichen), from 19 January 1935;
All with silver garland and darkened eagle, except Pilot/Observer badge, for which single-seat fighter pilots had to qualify:
(1) Pilot; *from 12 August 1935,* Pilot/Observer, gilt garland, silver eagle.
(2) Observer/Assistant Observer.
(3) Wireless Operator/Flight Engineer/Air Gunner; *from 22 June 1942,* Wireless Operator only.
(4) *From 22 June* 1942, Flight Engineer/Air Gunner
Mission clasps (Frontflugspangen), from 30 January 1941: Bronze for 20 operational flights, silver for 60, gold for 110.
(5) Day fighter, heavy fighter & ground attack; *from 13 May 1942,* day fighter only; *from 14 October 1942,* with black garland, night interceptor.
(6) *From 13 May 1942,* heavy fighter & ground attack; *from 14 October 1942,* with black garland, night intruder.
(7) Bomber, dive-bomber, transport & glider; *from 19 November 1941,* bomber & dive-bomber only. Illustrated with added pendant for gold clasp categories, *introduced 26 June 1942,* for 250 flights by recce & night fighter aircrew; 300 by bomber, air-sea rescue & weather; 400 by dive-bomber, heavy fighter & ground attack; 500 by day fighter & transport.
(8) *From 12 April 1944,* ground attack only. Illustrated with added pendant for all gold clasp categories, *introduced 29 April 1944,* numbered in 100-flight increments from 200 to 1,800. A unique diamond-studded '2,000' pendant was presented to Oberstleutnant Hans-Ulrich Rudel.
(9) *From 19 November 1941,* transport & glider only; flights drawing enemy fire counted double toward mission totals. *From 23 April 1942,* extended to on-board medical & signals personnel.
(10) Recce, air-sea rescue, weather.

Note: For 'battle badges' awarded to Luftwaffe personnel – including Flakartillerie – for ground and sea operations, see MAA 365, *World War II German Battle Insignia.*

OPPOSITE **France, 1940:** Ground crew wearing the lined dark blue or black *Arbeitsschutzanzug, geffütert.* The left hand man shows the buckled integral belt of the 1936 suit; the third from left has removed the belt altogether; and the second, fourth and fifth wear 1937 pattern overalls with the belt replaced by internal adjustment tapes. Note pocket details, neckerchiefs, and the use of high rubber boots by the two men at the right.

Generalmajor Galland at Ryelbitsii during a tour of fighter units on the Russian Front, winter 1942/43; he wears the pale natural sheepskin KW s/41 jacket. The accompanying Leutnant (left) and Hauptmann wear KW l/41 suits. Unusually, Galland is not smoking a cigar. As General der Jagdflieger he even officially granted himself permission to smoke on operations; long before he attained this rank his Bf109E was uniquely equipped with an electric lighter, salvaged from a car and fitted by his crew chief, Unteroffizier Gerhard Meyer. Three tobacco companies offered to supply the ace's 20-a-day habit; he graciously accepted all three. (Private collection)

D2: Leutnant, 2 Staffel/Nahaufklärungsgruppe 14; Libya, May 1942

Returned from a short range reconnaissance mission over Bir Hakeim, this Fi156C-3 'Storch' pilot wears the Tropenschirmmütze with button-on neck curtain, and first type Nitsche & Günther spectacle-style goggles. He has acquired Italian Army 'stivaletto coloniale' ankle boots and a bazaar-made tunic, worn over a zip-fronted civilian sweater. Added insignia include a pin-back metal breast eagle from the Sommeranzug. Note the scarce tropical Leibgurt (waist belt) with circular clasp buckle; and the shaped pockets for flare pistol and signal flag on the K So/41 trousers. Tan cloth examples were ideally suited, but far from exclusive to the Mediterranean theatre. The Luftwaffe cuff band 'AFRIKA', with grey-white cotton or aluminium-wire lettering on blue wool, was adopted from 25 February 1942. They were seldom worn in theatre, where repeated washing would damage insignia, and were usually reserved for continental uniform – assuming the wearer was fortunate enough to get home leave.

D3: Unterfeldwebel, 1 Staffel/Fernaufklärungsgruppe 122; Sardinia, February 1943

The combination of temperate and tropical clothing was characteristic of the Mediterranean theatre. This Waffenwart (ordnance specialist) wears the Fliegermütze 35 and Fliegerbluse 40 with tropical shorts rolled fashionably high. The popular and comfortable Laufschuhe are worn with issue grey socks. He reloads ammunition cans for a Bf109F-5 reconnaissance fighter with 500-round belts. It was vital to keep the rounds as clean as possible; any grit in a belt could foul the gun's feed, and many men were routinely employed in this laborious task – often undertaken on the wing root to avoid contact with the ground. His Gruppe, I./(F)122, flew long-range reconnaissance missions across the Mediterranean. (*Errata*: his shoulder straps should have *Tresse* across the ends.)

E: NORTH AFRICA & MEDITERRANEAN, 1942–44

E1: Feldwebel, Pioneer-Kompanie, Jagdgeschwader 27; Qasaba, North Africa, autumn 1942

Supervising construction of a 'Splitter-Büchse' (splinter box) three-sided protective pen of rock and sandbags for a Bf109F-2 of III./JG 27, the Feldwebel has donned a wool-knit Schlupfjacke 36 and Übermantel 35 against the evening chill.

Collar patches with laid-on 5mm Tresse sections were specific to NCOs' overcoats. This veteran 'Afrikakampfer', wears whipcord breeches and Tropen-Schnürstiefel boots with high integral strapped gaiters. Protective goggles with 'Umbral' 75–95 per cent tinted lenses give protection against sun and dust. Note the large, 1100ml (38fl.oz) Tropenfeldflasche with brown felt cover and webbing cradle [3]

E2: Gefreiter, Nachschubkompanie 14/Ersatzbataillon XI; Benghazi, 1942

Supply driver Wolf-Dieter Kerszebinsky, who arrived in Africa on 6 May 1942, is seen here bartering for souvenirs in an Arab bazaar. (German servicemen were typically paid on the 10th, 21st and 30th of each month, the Afrikakorps in Italian *lire*.) He wears Tropenanzug 41 as walking-out dress with Seitengewehr (bayonet), the prescribed sidearm, suspended from a webbing belt with sand-painted buckle. Use of the Tropenhelm was encouraged, though seldom enforced, between 08:00 and 16:00 hours when the sun was at its fiercest. According to Wehrmacht regulations, his camera is carried over the left shoulder when in public. Due to tropical insignia shortages he wears a continental Winkel and field-made Schulterklappen. Kerszebinsky received the Italian-German commemorative medal for Africa on 1 September 1942; was promoted to Obergefreiter on 1 May 1943; and one week later received the Iron Cross 2nd Class which was awarded as general issue upon surrender of the Afrikakorps. All had earned it.

E3: Leutnant, 5 Staffel/Jagdgeschwader 4; Ferrara, Italy, 1944

Stationed north-east of Bologna, this Fw190 pilot wears a well-shaped Sommermütze, a popular affectation in this climate, and displays the Knight's Cross with Oakleaves without the regulation necktie. From a previous victory against a 'Dicke Auto' ('fat car' – heavy bomber) he has acquired the prized USAAF A2 flyers' jacket, now adorned with his own shoulder boards. This is worn with tropical shorts, issue Tropen-Schnürschuhe and rolled white socks. A signalling mirror in its cloth cover is chained to his 10-30 B1 life vest, and a dye-marker pouch is tied to the waist strap. The mesh-topped Netzkopfhaube flight helmet was widely used in this theatre.

F: NORTHERN EUROPE, 1942–44

F1: Unteroffizier, 2 Staffel/Kampfgeschwader 200; Berlin-Finow, summer 1944

A 'Schwarze' prepares to re-spray a newly repaired Consolidated B-24J 'Liberator'. Activated from 20 February 1944, KG 200 was a special unit equipped with captured Allied aircraft for evaluation, fighter training, and some clandestine operations such as the dropping of agents. German-crewed B-17s and B-24s occasionally tagged onto USAAF formations posing as 'stragglers', to signal altitude, speed and course estimates to Flak batteries.

Partial Kragentresse on the collar points of his faded black Drillichbluse 35 is the only suggestion of rank. The separate cockade fitted to the Einheitsfliegermütze 43 tended to be obscured by its front flaps, and from early 1944

---

3 Collector's note: the phenol-resin type commonly referred to today as the tropical canteen was simply an economy version of the standard 800ml Feldflasche 31, and apparently saw no service in Africa whatsoever. It was frequently carried by Waffen-SS troops in Holland in 1944 (but this does not imply uniquely SS issue).

a new one-piece badge combined a smaller eagle and cockade on a trapezoidal backing.

F2: Oberleutnant, Ergänzungs Zerstörergruppe; Deblin-Irena, Poland, summer 1942

This Bf110E-1 instructor replenishes his stock of survival equipment carried in the versatile K So/41 flight trousers. In addition to the signal cartridges visible here, four could be housed in vertical dividers inside the left pocket, and two more in elastic loops under the flap of the right pocket. Cloth or steel anchoring loops were provided inside each knee pocket for cord equipment lanyards, one of which secures a 26.65mm Walther flare pistol to the integral holster. Yet more cartridges are carried in a Taille-Riemen, with longer types stored at the hips for the sake of comfort while seated. The jacket displays shoulder boards, Iron Cross 1st Class, and an embroidered cloth version of the Pilot/Observer's qualification badge. His Fliegerchronograph, on a lime green wrist strap, was made by Hanhart of Schwenningen-am-Neckar.

F3: Fähnrich, II Gruppe/ Zerstörergeschwader 76; Seerappen, East Prussia, autumn 1944

This keen young 'Nachwuchs' ('new growth', late war slang for a replacement pilot) on an Me410 squadron is equipped with the LKp N 101 helmet with two-strap oxygen mask fittings, and third type Nitsche & Günther Splitterschutzbrille with folding frames. He wears the jacket from a KW I/41 suit (with Swiss-made Ri-Ri plastic and steel zips), and trousers from the KW Fl bR/41 suit with ceramic central buttons added to knee pocket flaps. Although it could preclude use

with the aircraft's electrical circuit, such mismatches of wired and unwired items were commonplace. Note the soft orange rubber soles to his flying boots, and Ärmband-kompass 39 typically strapped to the 10-30 B2 life vest mouth tube.

G: EASTERN FRONT, 1943–45

G1: Flieger, 3 Staffel/Kampfgeschwader zbV 1; medical evacuation, Stalingrad, winter 1942/43

After off-loading desperately needed supplies at Pitomnik just outside Stalingrad, a 'Sanitäts-Ju' is hurriedly packed with as many casualties as possible for evacuation to Salk airfield. This assisting mechanic wears an M1937 blue denim one-piece lined working overall, and the awkward wooden-soled Filzschuhe over standard Schaftstiefel. In cold weather the wool Fliegermütze usually replaced the cotton drill cap, and is worn here over the wool-rayon toque. Braving the bitter conditions, it was common for aircrew to shed layers of heavy flight gear in an attempt to warm a few of their freezing casualties.

G2: Oberfeldwebel, II Gruppe/Schlacht-geschwader 2; Bögönd, Hungary, December 1944

Although rare by this date, the bulky KW I/33 suit remained popular with some for its warmth. The blue web belt and multi-panel boots are signs of late war economies. His clothing is completed by FW 5 m/33 gloves, and the Luftwaffe Bergmütze 38 – which was far from exclusive to Luftwaffe mountain service units. A carefully arranged Patronengurt is (unusually) worn around each ankle rather than the upper shins. When all five connecting eyes of the parachute harness were clicked home, the safety clip suspended from the right shoulder strap was snapped into a slot in the buckle housing, preventing accidental release. Removal of the clip, followed by a 90-degree clockwise turn and a sharp blow to the disc, immediately disengaged the connecting eyes and the harness fell away.

G3: Stabsgefreiter, Feldflugplatz-Abwehr; Mamaia, Romania, January 1945

Positioned to defend the north-eastern approaches to the base of II./ZG 1 and their Ju88A-14s, this man wears just the hood and trousers of the schwere Winteranzug, preferring a less restricting rabbitskin jacket. Felt-topped winter boots with separate toe and heel sections and civilian 'Winterhilfs' gloves complete his clothing, which is soiled with grease and carbon from the 8.8cm Flak-37. From September 1939 until the end of the war, all types of Flak-Kanone became increasingly engaged in the direct-fire ground role with great effect – most other nations dismissed the concept as too expensive.

Benghazi, Libya, 15 January 1942: a colonial Italian photographer made this portrait of Flieger Walter Schifer, wearing the smart and practical *Tropenanzug* with shafted boots, brown leather belt and K98k bayonet: cf Plate E2. His use of grey-blue wool shoulder straps from the continental uniform is indicative of the shortages that plagued the Afrikakorps. The tropical breast eagle applied during tunic manufacture was occasionally replaced with the more visible woollen variety. German servicemen often carried spare cloth insignia among their personal kit.

The most decorated German soldier in history: the Stuka pilot Major Hans-Ulrich Rudel of III./SG 2 'Immelmann', uniquely awarded – on 1 January 1945 – the Knight's Cross with Golden Oakleaves, Swords and Diamonds. He is photographed in Russia in 1944, with Feldwebel Bölling and Unteroffizier Maldinger, both unusually wearing partial *Kragentresse* on the *Fliegerbluse*, intended for work wear from 4 September 1942. Bolling's cloth braces support K So/41 trousers.

During more than 2,500 Ju87 sorties Rudel made 11 aerial 'kills', and destroyed 519 tanks and other AFVs (17 in one day), numerous bridges, railway junctions and soft-skinned vehicles, and sank a battleship, a cruiser, a destroyer and over 70 landing barges. Shot-up more than 30 times by artillery fire and wounded five times – once in the shoulder while escaping captivity (followed by a 50km walk back to safety) – he lost his right leg to a direct hit, but returned to combat within six weeks. (Private collection)

H: DEFENCE OF THE REICH, 1944–45
H1: Hauptmann, 12 Staffel/Nacht-jagdgeschwader 1; Leeuwarden, Holland, January 1944
This German-made black leather suit with zip-fastened pockets, worn here with a flamboyant neckerchief, was an expensive choice, and many chose not to adorn it with awards or even the breast eagle; here only the EK I and silver Frontflugspange für Nachtjäger are displayed. Aerial victories were an excuse for celebration, but privately most pilots could identify with their victims, increasing the strain on their nerves. It is remarkable how Luftwaffe airmen endured the accumulating mental pressures of their uniquely extended combat service.

H2: Oberhelferin, 2 Zug/Batterie 13, 14.Flakdivision; Leuna, Germany, October 1944
One of the few front-line postings open to German servicewomen was the Flakscheinwerferdienst (AA searchlight service), formed from 16 October 1943. This Höhenricht-kanonier illustrates standard field dress introduced in mid-1942: Skimütze, three-button Jackett with patch pockets and integral cloth belt, and tapered Keilhosen trousers with buttoned-flap pockets to hips and right rear, commonly tucked into grey socks. The IG Farben synthetic fuel refinery at Leuna, between Berlin and Frankfurt, produced some 75 million gallons (300,000 tons) of aviation grade fuel per year from high-pressure hydrogenisation of lignite coal; every ton of coal produced about 80 gallons.

This was the largest of 12 such plants, collectively supplying 85 per cent of Luftwaffe requirements. **Inset:** Embroidered Zugehörigkeitsabzeichen worn on the Kostümjacke, Jackett and Übermantel. (*Errata*: the cap eagle is wrongly shown as the reversed type.)

H3: Oberfahnrich, III Gruppe/Kampfgeschwader 76; Karstedt, Germany, 12 March 1945
Most operations in the final months were confined to home territory and the need for survival gear was much reduced. However, the leather KW/41 suit gave vital protection against the volatile J2 synthetic jet fuel – even relatively minor burns could induce rapid, and occasionally fatal blood poisoning. The myriad different uniforms encountered on German soil at this time necessitated quick identification to local inhabitants seeking revenge upon downed Allied 'Terrorflieger'; the screen-printed cotton armband – here slipped over the pocket flap – served this purpose. A well-worn enlisted ranks' Schirmmütze is fitted with officers' chin cords by this aspirant officer. KG 76 was heavily engaged against the Allied Rhine crossings, and this man awaits preparation of his Arado Ar234B-2 jet bomber for an 18-plane level attack on the Ludendorff bridge at Remagen, held by US 9th Armored Division. The raid, and another the next day, proved fruitless. Such operations were considered 'Himmelfahrtskommando' ('heaven-bound', i.e. suicide missions).

March 1945: captured near Berstadt by the US 4th Armored Division, this Flakhelferin wears the *Skimütze* without *Reichskokarde*, and a *Jackett* echoing the Army's *Feldbluse 44*, fitted with the *Zugehörigkeitsabzeichen* on the right upper sleeve – see Plate H' Some women alternatively received standard mens' *Fliegerblusen*. Ten operators served each 110 volt/24 kilowatt *Flakscheinwerfer* 150cm searchlight and associated equipment (nine per battery). Under a Scheinwerferführer, they were numbered according to duties: H1, Höhen-richtkanonier (elevation operator); H2, Leuchtkanonier (assistant light operator); H3, Lampenwart (lamp engineer); H4, Beobachter (observer); H5, Sieten-Richtkanonier (traverse operator); H6, Maschinist (mechanical engineer); H7 & H8, Horchgeräten-Arbeiter (sound-detector operators); and H9, Fern-sprecher/ Fernschreiber (communications operator). (US Army Signal Corps)

INDEX

Figures in **bold** refer to illustrations